THE LAW
(IN PLAIN ENGLISH)®
FOR HEALTH CARE
PROFESSIONALS

Other books by Leonard D. DuBoff:

The Law (in Plain English)® for Craftspeople
Business and Legal Forms (in Plain English)® for Craftspeople
The Law (in Plain English)® for Small Businesses
The Law (in Plain English)® for Writers
The Photographers' Business and Legal Handbook
The Book Publishers' Legal Guide
The Desk Book of Art Law
Art Law in a Nutshell
Law and the Visual Arts
Art Law: Domestic and International
High-Tech Law (in Plain English)®: An Entrepreneur's Guide
The Crafts Business Encyclopedia

THE LAW
(IN PLAIN ENGLISH)®
FOR HEALTH CARE
PROFESSIONALS

Leonard D. DuBoff

**Foreword by Kirk Johnson,
General Counsel & Senior Vice President
American Medical Association**

John Wiley & Sons, Inc.
New York • Chichester • Brisbane

Toronto • Singapore

Library of Congress Cataloging-in-Publication Data:

DuBoff, Leonard D.
   The law (in plain English) for health care professionals / by
Leonard D. DuBoff ; foreword by Kirk Johnson.
      p.   cm.
   Includes index.
   ISBN 0-471-58001-5 (cloth).— ISBN 0-471-58002-3 (paper)
1. Law—United States.   2. Medical care—Law and legislation—
United States.   3. Physicians—United States—Handbooks, manuals,
etc.   4. Dentists—United States—Handbooks, manuals, etc.
I. Title
KF390.P45D83   1993
349.73′02461—dc20
[347.3002461]   92-39745

Printed in the United States of America

10   9   8   7   6   5   4   3   2   1

To
My wife, Mary Ann Crawford DuBoff,
a registered nurse and legal assistant;
My mother, Millicent Barbara DuBoff;
and
to the memories of my sister,
Candise DuBoff-Jones,
and
My aunt, Sylvia Pessah.

Contents

Foreword

It is well recognized that the quality of medical care in the United States is generally excellent. Our medical schools and teaching hospitals provide medical practitioners with the most up-to-date and accurate medical information available. While it is clear that the profession strives to equip health care professionals with the best medical skills possible, until now less has been done to provide the practitioner with the fundamental business skills necessary to operate a modern medical practice.

In this book, Leonard D. DuBoff, a Professor of Law and practicing business attorney, discusses important business issues that are relevant to a modern medical practice. From questions of business forms, including tax considerations, to record retention and disclosure, this text is intended to assist doctors and other licensed medical professionals in understanding the many legal and business issues encountered in their practices. Employment contracts, advertising, insurance, pension and profit sharing, estate planning, and a host of other relevant subjects are also covered "(in Plain English)®." It is intended to provide the reader with a very understandable analysis of the law for the purpose of instituting preventative business practices that are likely to result in fewer legal problems.

The author makes it clear that this book is not a substitute for a lawyer but, instead, is designed to aid the reader in working with an attorney. It is a book that is a welcome addition to the medical practitioner's library and one that will add a good deal of practical business knowledge to the literature available for the medical profession.

KIRK JOHNSON
General Counsel &
Senior Vice President
American Medical Association
Chicago, Illinois

Acknowledgments

The task of assembling, analyzing, and digesting the huge volume of legal material that affects licensed medical and dental professionals could not have been undertaken without the support and assistance of numerous individuals. While it would be impossible to identify all of them, there are some who deserve special recognition. I would, therefore, like to thank my friends, colleagues, clients, students, and former students for all of their help, and in particular, Brent Crew, J.D., Lewis and Clark Law School, 1992; Lynn Della, my former legal assistant; Thomas E. Cooney, Sr., Senior Partner, and Michael D. Crew, Partner, of the law firm of Cooney & Crew, P.C.; and many of the other lawyers in that firm including Connie E. McKelvy, and Raymond F. Mensing, Jr., former Vice President/General Counsel for the Oregon Association of Hospitals. My colleague, Professor Larry Brown of Lewis and Clark Law School, provided me with valuable comments and insights in the area of tax law, as did William Parkhurst of the accounting firm of Yergen & Meyer, Bonnie Parsons of the accounting firm of Hoffmaster & Grinage, and Joe Markunas, C.P.A. I would also like to thank Lenair Mulford for performing the yeoman's task of converting my incomprehensible notes, interlineations, and pieces of scrap paper into a coherent manuscript and Ormond H. Ormsby for his help with the materials on pensions and profit sharing. My literary agent, Elizabeth Wales of the firm of Levant and Wales, also deserves thanks for her help in obtaining an excellent arrangement for the publication of this book, as well as PJ Dempsey, Senior Editor at John Wiley & Sons for her support, insight, and confidence with respect to this project.

I would like to applaud the help of my three children, Colleen Rose DuBoff, Robert Courtney DuBoff, and Sabrina Ashley DuBoff, for their understanding and cooperation when it was necessary for me to forgo participating in their activities in order to work on this volume. Finally, I would like to once again acknowledge the incredible work of my partner in law and in life for the past 25 years, Mary Ann DuBoff, in helping me complete this task. She has continued to provide me with the necessary assistance in order to convert the idea of a business counseling tool for medical professionals into this volume.

This volume is another in the series I started many years ago of law books that are intended to educate nonlawyers. *The Law (in Plain English)*® series contains books for small businesses, writers, craftspeople, photographers, artists, and now licensed medical and dental professionals. It is hoped that this volume will be as successful in providing nonlawyers with the information necessary to effectively practice their chosen profession as the other volumes in this series have been.

Introduction

For some time, friends, relatives, and clients who are medical professionals made it clear to me that there was a need for a book that would aid them in understanding the myriad of business problems they encounter on a regular basis. All felt confident with respect to their medical skills but when it came to structuring their profession as a business, they felt somewhat insecure. Professional schools rarely provide the kind of education that will enable a graduate to properly structure a practice so as to achieve the maximum protection afforded by the law while deriving the maximum business benefits possible.

While professionals such as lawyers and accountants are available to assist a medical or dental practitioner with the complex business, tax, and other legal issues that arise in practice, still it is not always clear when help is needed until a situation has so deteriorated as to be irretrievable. In addition, if one takes certain precautions and is careful to provide the proper foundation for necessary business transactions, many difficulties can be avoided.

As a law professor for more than two decades, I have learned the importance of preproblem counseling. I have advised my students that it is important for them to service their clients by using all possible methods of avoiding costly and time-consuming litigation. Unfortunately, our legal system is quite complex and is constantly changing. It is often quite difficult to identify potential legal problems and to avoid becoming entangled in litigation.

The purpose of this text is to provide the licensed medical or dental professional with a single readable volume that will assist in identifying most of the legal issues to be evaluated and competently dealt with by them in their practice. The primary focus of this book is on the business of being a licensed medical or dental professional. Each of the subjects considered could actually support a multivolume treatise as well as a law school course. Many do and, therefore, the treatment here is of necessity quite general. It is hoped that you will use this book to sensitize you to the variety of issues to be discussed with your attorney, accountant, or other business advisor.

While there is a chapter devoted to professional liability, that is not the primary focus of this book. It is included because it is one of the many issues encountered by medical and dental practitioners, and any book that purports to serve as a business counseling tool would be incomplete without such a discussion. Most professional associations have books, pamphlets, and videos aimed more directly at professional liability, and it is essential for you to continue to update your knowledge regarding the problems that can and do arise in your specialty.

1

Organizing Your Business

Everyone in business, and professionals are engaged in business, knows that survival requires careful financial planning. Yet few fully realize the importance of selecting the best *form* for the business. Professional businesses have little need for the sophisticated organizational structures utilized in industry, but since all professionals must pay taxes, obtain loans, and expose themselves to potential liability on a regular basis, it only makes sense to structure one's business so as to minimize these concerns.

Every business has an organizational form best suited to it. When I counsel people on organizing their businesses, I usually adopt a two-step approach.

First, we discuss various aspects of taxes and liability in order to decide which of the basic forms is best. There are only a handful of basic forms available for doctors, dentists, and other medical professionals: the *sole proprietorship*, the *partnership*, and the *professional corporation* (hereinafter PC).

Second, once we have decided which of these is appropriate, we go into the organizational details such as partnership agreements or corporate documents. These documents define the day-to-day operations of a business and therefore must be tailored to individual situations.

What I offer here is an explanation of the features of each kind of organization, including advantages and disadvantages. This should give you some idea of which form might be best for you.

I will discuss potential problems but, since I cannot go into a full discussion of the more intricate details, you should consult an attorney before deciding to adopt any particular structure. My purpose here is to facilitate your communication with your lawyer and to enable you to better understand the choices offered.

The American Dream: Sole Proprietorship

The technical name *sole proprietorship* may be unfamiliar to you, but the notion of a country doctor working in a home office is a classic example. The sole proprietorship is an unincorporated business owned by one person. Though not peculiar to the United States, it was, and still is, the backbone of the American dream, to the extent that personal freedom follows economic freedom. As a form of business it is elegant in its simplicity. All it requires is a little money and much work. Legal requirements are few and simple. In most localities, you must obtain a business license from the city or county for a small fee. If you wish to operate the business under a name other than your own, the name must be registered with the state and, in some cases, the county in which you are doing business. In addition, you of course must have a license to practice your chosen profession, and your profession must permit you to act independently. With these details taken care of, you are in business.

Disadvantages of Sole Proprietorship

There are many financial risks involved in operating your business as a sole proprietor. If you recognize any of these dangers as a real threat, you probably should consider an alternative form of organization.

If you are the sole proprietor of a business venture, the property you personally own is at stake. In other words, if for any reason you owe more than the dollar value of your business, your creditors can force a sale of most of your nonbusiness property to satisfy the debt.

For many risks, insurance is available that will shift the loss from you to an insurance company, but there are some risks for which insurance is simply not available. In addition, the cost of professional liability has become so high that many medical professionals have been forced to change careers. Even when procured, every insurance policy has a limited, strictly defined scope of coverage. These liability risks, as well as many other uncertain economic factors, can drive a small business, and thus the sole proprietor, into bankruptcy.

Taxes for the Sole Proprietor

The sole proprietor is taxed on all profits of the business and may deduct losses. Of course, the rate of taxation will change with increases in income. Fortunately, there are ways to ease this tax burden. For instance, you can establish an approved IRA or pension plan, deducting a specified amount of your net income for placement into the pension plan, into an interest-bearing account, or into approved government securities or mutual funds to be withdrawn later when you are in a lower tax bracket. There are severe restrictions, however, on withdrawal of this money prior to retirement age.

For further information on tax planning devices, you should contact your local IRS office and ask for free pamphlets. Or you might wish to use the services of an accountant or attorney experienced in dealing with business-tax planning. (See also Chapter 14.)

Partnership

A *partnership* is defined by most state laws as an association of two or more persons who conduct, as co-owners, a business for profit. No formalities are required. In fact, in some cases people have been held to be partners even though they never had any intention of forming a partnership. For example, if you lend a friend some money to start a business and the friend agrees to pay you a certain percentage of whatever profit is made, you may be your friend's partner in the eyes of the law even though you take no part in running the business. This is important because each partner is subject to unlimited personal liability for the debts of the partnership. Also, each partner is liable for the negligence of another partner and of the partnership's employees when a negligent act occurs in the usual course of business. In effect, each partner is considered an employee of the partnership.

This means that if you are getting involved in a partnership, you should be especially cautious in two areas. First, since the involvement of a partner increases your potential liability, you should choose a responsible partner. Second, the partnership should be adequately insured to protect both the assets of the partnership and the personal assets of each partner.

As I have already mentioned, no formalities are required to create a partnership. If the partners do not have a formal agreement defining the terms of the partnership—such as control of the partnership or the distribution of profits—state law will determine the terms. State laws are based on the fundamental characteristics of the typical partnership as it has existed throughout the ages and are therefore thought to correspond to the reasonable expectations of the partners. The most important of these legally presumed characteristics are:

1. No one can become a member of a partnership without the unanimous consent of all partners;

2. All members have an equal vote in the management of the partnership regardless of the size of their interest in it;

3. All partners share equally in the profits and losses of the partnership no matter how much capital they have contributed;

4. A simple majority vote is required for decisions in the ordinary course of business, and a unanimous vote is required to change the fundamental character of the business; and

5. A partnership is terminable at will by any partner; a partner can withdraw from the partnership at any time, and this withdrawal will cause a dissolution of the partnership.

Most state laws contain a provision that allows the partners to make their own agreements regarding the management structure and division of profits that best suits the needs of the individual partners.

What You Don't Want: Unintended Partners

One arrangement you want to avoid is the unintended partnership. This can occur when you work together with another person and your relationship is not described formally. There are cases in which professionals have been held liable for the acts of other independent professionals where it appeared to third persons that they were partners when in fact they were not. In *Hill v. St. Clare's Hospital* (67 N.Y.S.2d 72, 499 N.Y.S.2d 904, 490 N.E.2d 823 (1986)), a patient sought medical care from a physician who conducted an independent practice but rendered services along with other physicians under a common name. When the care rendered was deemed negligent, the patient sued. It was held that all of the physicians doing business under the common name were liable as if they were partners despite the fact that there was merely an office-sharing arrangement. Important to the court were the facts that the physicians conducted their practice under a common name, had a consolidated accounting system including billing, a single letterhead listing all of the physicians who shared space in the office, a single phone number that was answered in a clinic name, and a clinic bank account out of which each independent physician drew amounts due for work performed.

To minimize this kind of exposure, medical professionals who merely share office space should take care to avoid using a common name. They should post a sign in their waiting room making it clear that individuals in the office practice independently from one another in treating their own patients and are not members of a group practice. Each medical professional should have a different phone number from the other practitioners that should be answered by using that particular professional's name. If a single number is desired, then a more generic greeting such as "Physicians' Offices" or the like should be used. Each practitioner should have a separate bank account and render his or her billings on an individualized letterhead. A consolidated letterhead should never be used. Again, care should be taken to avoid giving the impression that the individual practitioners are engaged in any form of group practice. Patient charts should be separated, and each practitioner should prepare an individualized fee schedule. Patients should be provided with a written notice similar to that which appears in the waiting room as part of their signed intake form.

Professional Corporation

The word "corporation" generally calls to mind a vision of a large company with hundreds of employees. One generally does not associate a corporation with a private medical practice. Traditionally, corporations could not "practice a profession." But since the late 1960s states have been enacting legislation that permits individuals licensed to practice a profession to form a corporation for the practice of that profession. This adaptation of the standard business corporation is called a "professional corporation" or "PC."

The general incorporation statutes used by most businesses are not available for professionals such as doctors, dentists, and other licensed medical professionals. Similarly, the not-for-profit corporation, which is a common organizational structure for hospitals, is also not available for professionals as a vehicle for practicing their profession. If these individuals desire to incorporate for the purpose of practicing medicine, dentistry, or the like, they may only set up a professional corporation.

There are advantages and disadvantages to incorporating your medical practice; if it appears advantageous to incorporate, you will find it can be done with surprising ease and with little expense. However, you will need a lawyer's assistance to ensure compliance with state formalities, instruction on corporate mechanics, and advice on corporate taxation.

Differences between a Professional Corporation and a Partnership

To better understand the professional corporation, it is useful to compare it to a partnership. Perhaps the most important difference is that the owners of the PC, commonly known as shareholders or stockholders, *generally* are not personally liable for the PC's debts; they stand to lose only their investment in the corporation. A shareholder is allowed full participation in the control of the PC through the shareholder's voting privileges.

Liability Limited liability is, however, something of an illusion. Very often creditors will require that the owner/shareholders personally co-sign for any credit extended. More importantly, incorporating will not protect an individual from liability for his or her own acts of malpractice; individuals remain responsible for their own wrongful acts. Thus, a shareholder who is found guilty of professional negligence (malpractice, wrongful conduct, etc.) will not only subject the corporation to liability, but also remains personally liable. All of the shareholder's personal assets (for example, house and car) are at risk to satisfy the judgment against him or her.

Where one shareholder is guilty of negligence or misconduct, most state statutes limit the other shareholders' liability to their investment in the PC. But, a minority of states hold all shareholders liable for each other's professional liability or misconduct. In other words, if one shareholder is found guilty of malpractice, *all* shareholders can be held personally liable to satisfy the judgment. In these few states, the other shareholders' liability remains limited with regard to other potential exposures such as debts and other contractual obligations.

The "corporate shield" also offers protection in situations where an agent hired by the PC has committed a wrongful act while working for the corporation. If, for example, a receptionist negligently injures a pedestrian while driving somewhere on corporate business, the employee will be liable for the wrongful act and the PC *may* be liable, but the shareholders who own the PC will probably not be personally liable.

Continuity of Existence   The second major difference between a PC and a partnership relates to continuity of existence. Since there is often a frequent turnover of members in group practice, this is an important factor. The many events that can cause the dissolution of a partnership do not have the same effect on a corporation. In fact, most corporations are created having perpetual existence. Unlike partners, shareholders cannot decide to withdraw and demand a return of capital from the corporation; all they can do is sell their stock. Therefore, a corporation may have both legal and economic continuity. This can also be a tremendous disadvantage to shareholders or their heirs if they want to sell stock when there are no buyers for it. However, agreements can be made about, and some state statutes require, a return of capital to the estate of a shareholder who dies or to a shareholder who decides to withdraw.

Transferability of Ownership   The third difference relates to transferability of ownership. In a partnership, no one can become a partner without unanimous consent of the other partners, unless otherwise agreed. In a PC, however, shareholders can generally sell part or all of their shares to qualified purchasers without the others' consent though there are a handful of states that do require shareholder approval before sale.

There is a significant limitation to the transfer of stock ownership that is common throughout most states, with the exception of Oregon and Louisiana. The purchaser of the shares must be a licensed member of the profession. There are some qualifications to this limitation that vary from state to state. In the majority of states, the shareholders need not be employees. Rhode Island and Colorado do require that shareholders also be employees. In New York, shareholders must be former or present employees of the PC, or individuals who will be employees within 30 days of the issuance of shares to them. Some states do allow the PC to consist of a combination of licensed health care professionals. For example, the shareholders of the PC may consist of doctors, nurses, dentists, and other medical professionals. But most states allow the PC to render only one type of professional service—medical care only or dental care only. A handful of state corporate statutes permit a crossover of professional services. Yet, even in these states, the licensing boards may prohibit the blending of medical professionals with other professionals. For example, lawyers or accountants are customarily not permitted to own stock in medical PCs.

In Oregon and Louisiana, shareholders may be nonprofessionals though their rights as shareholders are limited. In Louisiana, nonprofessional shareholders may not vote or otherwise participate in the earnings or affairs of the PC. Nonprofessional shareholders are allowed to be directors and/or officers of the PC in Oregon, under its Professional Corporation Code, as long as at least 51 percent of the shareholders and directors of the PC are licensed within the PC specialty.

An issue related to the transferability of ownership is the involuntary transfer of shares. More specifically, what happens to a shareholder's stock when he or she dies? Once again, the laws vary from state to state. With the exception of Iowa, Washington, and Pennsylvania (where state law essentially compels the deceased shareholder's shares to be turned over to the corporation for a specified amount), the matter of disposition of shares upon death may be covered in the articles of incorporation, bylaws, or in shareholder agreements, commonly called buy–sell agreements. Some states require that the professional corporation code be consulted to determine any limitations on the content of the provisions or agreement (such as first rights of refusal). Regardless of how the disposition is provided for, the shares must be transferred to a "qualified" shareholder within a specified period of time (90 days to 13 months). Consequently, the new shareholder must still meet the particular state's shareholder requirements previously discussed.

By far the most common source for determining the procedure for disposition of shares upon death is the buy–sell agreement. The buy–sell agreement commits the seller and the buyer (either the corporation or the other shareholders) to the sale of shares at a fixed or readily determinable price prior to the shareholder's death. Valuation of shares in a PC is quite complex, thus the aid of a skilled attorney, accountant, or business appraiser is highly advised.

Since shares in a PC are not tradeable per se and can generally only be transferred to other licensed professionals, the buy–sell agreement is a very important planning device. For the shareholder, it clarifies the transaction prior to death and provides liquidity for a deceased shareholder's estate. It may also fix the value of the stock for estate tax purposes. For the remaining shareholders in the PC, the buy–sell agreement prevents the seller from transferring stock to an unacceptable outsider and ensures that legal and ethical requirements are met.

If a buy–sell agreement is not used, provisions can be made for the disposition of shares in the articles of incorporation or bylaws. In the event that no provision is made for the disposition of shares upon a shareholder's death, state law determines the procedure for disposition. Most of the state laws that require a corporate repurchase of the stock set the price at "book value." Per share book value is the net worth of the PC (assets minus debts) divided by the number of shares outstanding. Often, the book value may not represent a fair value for the stock, since goodwill, reputation, and other intangible factors and the true worth of assets may not be accurately reflected. Generally accepted accounting principles would permit real estate to be carried on the PC's books at its cost less depreciation. Similarly, marketable securities may be carried on the books at cost rather than at current value. Goodwill is not reflected on a PC's balance sheet unless the business, including good will, was purchased from another. Consequently, it is wiser for the shareholders themselves to provide a method for the disposition of shares that includes a formula for valuation.

Management and Control   The fourth difference between PCs and partnerships is in the structure of management and control. Common shareholders are given a vote in proportion to their ownership in the professional corporation. Other kinds of stock can be created, with or without voting rights. The shareholders elect the board of directors, who in turn make policy decisions for the PC.

The basic rules of the PC are stated in the articles of incorporation, which are filed with the state and which, in essence, read the state professional corporation law into them. These serve as a sort of constitution, and can generally only be amended by shareholder vote. More detailed operational rules—bylaws—should also be prepared. Both shareholders and directors may have the power to create or amend bylaws. Control over bylaws varies from state to state and may be determined by the shareholders themselves. The board of directors then makes operational decisions for the corporation and might delegate day-to-day operations to a president.

A shareholder, even one who owns all the stock, may not preempt a decision of the board of directors. If the board has exceeded the powers granted it by the articles or bylaws, a shareholder may obtain a court order remedying the situation. But if the board is within its powers, the shareholders have no recourse except to remove the entire board or a specific board member. However, since the shareholders most commonly *are* the board members in a PC, this is rarely a problem.

In a few states, a professional corporation may entirely forgo having a board of directors. In such cases, the corporation is authorized to allow the shareholders to vote directly on business decisions just as in a partnership.

Tax   The last distinction between professional corporations and partnerships is taxation. Doctors, dentists, and other professionals used to form PCs in order to obtain significant corporate tax advantages unavailable to the self-employed. The major tax advantage was a deferral of taxes through contributions to qualified corporation pensions and profit-sharing plans. But in 1982, the Tax Equity and Fiscal Responsibility Act eliminated this advantage by granting a similar tax deferral to the self-employed.

There remains a further distinction in the way a PC is taxed. Under both state and federal laws, the profits of the corporation are taxed to the corporation before they are paid out as dividends. Then, because the dividends constitute income to the shareholders, they are taxed again as personal income. This double taxation constitutes the major disadvantage of incorporating.

AVOIDING DOUBLE TAXATION OF CORPORATE INCOME

There are several methods of avoiding double taxation. First, a PC can plan its business so as not to show very much profit. This can be done by drawing off what would be profit in payments to shareholders in other capacities. For example, a shareholder can be paid a salary, rent for property leased to the corporation, or interest on a loan made to the PC. All of these are legal deductions from corporate income.

The PC can also get larger deductions for the various health and retirement benefits provided for its employees than can a sole proprietor or a partnership. For example, a PC can deduct all of its payments made for an employee health plan while at the same time the employee does not pay any personal income tax on this. Sole proprietors or partnerships may only deduct a much smaller portion of these expenses.

The PC can also reinvest its profits for reasonable business expansion. This undistributed money is not taxed as income to the individual as it would be if earned by a sole proprietor or partnership, which does not distribute it.

Reinvestment has two advantages. First, the business can be built up with money that has been taxed only at the corporate level and on which no individual shareholder needs to pay any tax. Second, the owners can delay the liquidation and distribution of corporate assets until a time of lower personal income and therefore lower tax rates.

In addition to the problem of double taxation, there is the *minor* possibility that the PC may be regarded by the IRS as a "personal holding company" and be taxed at 28 percent on any "undistributed personal holding company income" in addition to any ordinary income tax. However, with the help of a good tax lawyer or CPA, some precautionary measures, and a little creativity, the pitfalls of double taxation and the personal holding company can be avoided or at least minimized.

Requirements for Incorporation

There are some preliminary "housekeeping" requirements that are necessary to form a PC. For example, articles of incorporation will need to be drafted and filed with the appropriate state and, in some states, local authorities, bylaws need to be written up, and the necessary fees must be paid. Most of these will require the aid of an attorney.

In addition to the creation formalities, there are other requirements that must be fulfilled during the life of the PC. To obtain and retain the benefits of corporate status, the PC must be identified as a legal entity separate from the individual practitioners. This means that certain corporate formalities must be strictly adhered to. A board of directors' meeting should be held at least annually and documented by written minutes. A shareholder meeting should also be held at least annually and be documented. Shareholders and directors must be careful not to commingle their private funds with corporate funds nor use corporate funds for their own personal purposes. A separate bank account should be opened for the PC to facilitate the separation of corporate from noncorporate funds.

The name of the corporation generally must include the last name of one or more of the shareholders (unless the particular state law permits something different) followed by the words "Professional Corporation" or the abbreviation "Prof. Corp." or simply "P.C." Such seemingly trivial things as posting a sign with the company name (with P.C. designation) at the place of business and printing stationery and business cards with the corporate name will help to ensure that the practice is characterized as a professional corporation.

The consequences of failing to observe corporate formalities or of commingling private and corporate assets may not be immediately apparent. However, if a creditor, patient, or other third party tries to enforce a corporate debt or obligation, a court may look beyond the corporation to the shareholders and impose unlimited personal liability for the debt or obligation. In other words, the benefit of limited liability, when available, may be forfeited if the shareholders fail to observe the formal requirements for the corporation.

Precautions for Minority Shareholders

Dissolving a corporation is not only painful because of certain tax penalties, it is frequently impossible without the consent of the majority of the shareholders. If you are involved in the formation of a corporation and will be a minority shareholder, you must realize that the majority will have ultimate and absolute control unless minority shareholders take certain precautions from the start. Avoiding these problems is no more difficult than drafting an agreement similar to a partnership agreement among the shareholders. It is wise to retain your own attorney to represent you during the corporation's formation rather than waiting until a problem arises.

It is important to determine which business form will be most advantageous for you. This can best be done by consulting with an experienced business lawyer and having your situation evaluated.

In the next chapter, I have prepared some questions you may wish to answer before meeting with your attorney. This should help minimize the amount of attorney's time necessary to create your new business entity.

2

Organizational Checklist

The process of creating a partnership or professional corporation is not particularly complex, but it is worthwhile having an experienced attorney and/or accountant assist you with tax planning and in preparing the necessary documents. In order to maximize your efficiency when dealing with these professionals, the checklists contained in this chapter should be used as a guide. Once you have obtained the necessary information, you and your professionals will be in a better position to determine the most appropriate organizational structure for your practice.

Major Items of a Partnership Agreement

Some of the major considerations in preparing a partnership agreement include the name of the partnership, a description of the business, contributions of capital by the partners, duration of the partnership, distribution of profits, management responsibilities, duties of partners, prohibited acts, and provisions for the dissolution of the partnership.

As you can see, a comprehensive partnership agreement is no simple matter. It is, in fact, essential for potential partners to devote some time and considerable care to the preparation of an agreement and to enlist the services of a business lawyer. The expense of a lawyer to help you put together an agreement suited to the needs of your partnership is usually well justified by the economic savings in the smooth organization, operation, and, when necessary, final dissolution of the partnership.

The economic advantages of doing business in a partnership form are the pooling of capital, collaboration of skills, easier access to credit enhanced by the collective credit rating, and a potentially more efficient allocation of labor and resources. A major disadvantage is that each partner is fully and personally liable for all the debts of the partnership, even if not personally involved in incurring those debts.

Taxes

A partnership does not possess any special tax advantages over a sole proprietorship. Each partner pays tax on his or her share of the profits, whether distributed or retained, and each is entitled to the same proportion of the partnership deductions and credits. The partnership must prepare for the IRS an annual information return known as Schedule K-1, Form 1065, which details each partner's share of income, credits, and deductions and against which the IRS can check the individual returns filed by the partners.

The Eight Basics of a Partnership Agreement

The Name of the Partnership

Most partnerships simply use as names the surnames of the major partners. The choice in that case is nothing more than the order of names, which depends on various factors from prestige to the way the names sound. If a name other than those of the partners is used, it will be necessary to file the assumed business name with the state. Care should be taken to choose a name that is distinctive and not already in use. If the name is not distinctive, others can copy it; if the name is already in use, you could be liable for trade-name infringement.

A Description of the Business

In describing their business, the partners should agree on the basic scope of the business—its requirements in regard to capital and labor, the parties' individual contributions of capital and labor, and perhaps some plans regarding future growth.

Partnership Capital

After determining how much capital to contribute, the partners must decide when it will be contributed, how to value the property contributed, and whether there is to be a right to contribute more or to withdraw any at a later date.

Duration of the Partnership

Sometimes partnerships are organized for a fixed amount of time or are automatically dissolved on certain conditions, such as the completion of a project.

Distribution of Profits

You can make whatever arrangement you want for distribution. Although ordinarily a partner does not receive a salary, it is possible to give an active partner a guaranteed salary in addition to a share of the profits. Since the partnership's profits can be determined only at the close of a business year, ordinarily no distribution is made until that time. However, it is possible to allow the partners a monthly draw of money against their final share of profits. In some cases it may be necessary to allow limited expense accounts for some partners.

Not all of the profits of the partnership need to be distributed at year's end. Some can be retained for expansion, an arrangement that can be provided for in the partnership agreement. Note, though, that whether the profits are distributed or not, all partners must pay tax on their shares. The tax code refers directly to the partnership agreement to determine what that share is, which shows how important a partnership agreement is.

Management

The division of power in the partnership can be made in many ways. All partners can be given an equal voice, or some more than others. A few partners might be allowed to manage the business entirely, the remaining partners being given a vote only on specifically designated areas of concern. Besides voting, three other areas of management should be covered. First is the question of who can sign checks, place orders, or enter into contracts on behalf of the partnership. Under state partnership laws any partner may do these things so long as they are in the usual course of business. But such a broad delegation of authority can lead to confusion, so it might be best to delegate this authority more narrowly.

Second, it is a good idea to determine a regular date for partnership meetings. Third, some consideration should be given to the possibility of a disagreement among the partners that leads to a deadlock. One way to avoid this is to distribute the voting power in such a way as to make a deadlock impossible. However, in a two-person partnership this would mean that one partner would be in absolute control. This might be unacceptable to the other partner. If, instead, the power is divided evenly among an even number of partners, as is often the case, the agreement should stipulate a neutral party or arbitrator who could settle any dispute and thereby avoid a dissolution of the partnership.

Prohibited Acts

By law, each partner owes the partnership certain duties by virtue of being an employee or agent of the partnership. First is the duty of diligence. This means the partner must exercise reasonable care in acting as a partner. Second is a duty of obedience. The partner must obey the rules of the partnership and, most importantly, must not exceed the authority that the partnership has vested in him or her. Finally, there is a duty of loyalty. A partner may not, without approval of the other partners, compete with the partnership in another business. A partner may not seize upon a business opportunity that would be of value to the partnership without first telling the partnership about it and allowing the partnership to pursue it.

A list of acts prohibited to any partner should be made a part of the partnership agreement, elaborating and expanding on these acts.

Dissolution and Liquidation

A partnership is automatically dissolved upon the death, withdrawal, or expulsion of a partner. Dissolution identifies the legal end of the partnership but need not affect its economic life if the partnership agreement has provided for the continuation of the business after a dissolution. Nonetheless, a dissolution will affect the business because the partner who withdraws or is expelled, or the estate of the deceased partner, will be entitled to a return of the proportionate share of capital that the departing partner contributed. Details such as how this capital will be returned should be decided before dissolution, because at the time of dissolution it may be impossible to negotiate. One method of handling this is to provide for a return of the capital in cash over a period of time. Some provision should be made so that the remaining partners will know how much of a departing partner's interest they may purchase.

After a partner leaves, the partnership may need to be reorganized and recapitalized. Again, provision for this should be worked out in advance, if possible. Finally, since it is always possible that the partners will eventually want to liquidate the partnership, it should be decided in advance who will liquidate the assets, which assets will be distributed, and what property will be returned to its original contributor.

Incorporation

As discussed in the previous chapter, there are usually two reasons for incorporation: limiting personal liability in some situations and minimizing federal income tax liability. The second reason is generally applicable to a practice that is earning a good deal of money. Even if you are not in that category, you may nevertheless want to consider incorporating in order to limit your personal liability.

Corporations are hypothetical legal people and, as such, are responsible for their own acts and contracts, although, as discussed in the preceding chapter, in many states professional corporations may not shield the practitioner from professional liability. Thus, if the professional corporation neglects to pay for materials ordered by it, if the corporation's receptionist negligently injures a pedestrian while on company business, or if a patient is injured by tripping in the professional corporation's waiting room, the professional corporation, not its owners, will be liable if the proper formalities have been followed. It should be noted that any individual personally responsible for a wrongful act will also be liable and, in some states, the practitioner may also be liable for acts of malpractice.

Incorporating is generally a fairly simple matter, but to do it right and utilize all the advantages, it is highly recommended that you consult a lawyer. A lawyer's time, of course, is money, but you can save some of that money if you come properly prepared. Following are some important points you will need to discuss with your lawyer.

Certified Public Accountant (CPA)

Other than yourself, the most important person with whom your attorney will work is your accountant. The accountant will provide valuable input on the professional corporation's financial structure, funding, capitalization, allocation of stock, and so forth. Your lawyer will be looking to your accountant to provide an opening balance sheet for the professional corporation from the time that the business moves from sole proprietorship or partnership to corporate status.

Corporate Name

Contact your attorney ahead of time with the proposed name of the professional corporation. A quick phone call or inquiry to the Corporation Commissioner, Division of Corporations, or Secretary of State in your state capital will reveal whether the proposed corporate name is available. Your attorney can reserve your chosen corporate name until you are ready to use it. You will also have to consider whether the corporation will have a special mark or logo that needs federal trademark protection or state registration.

Corporate Structure

Who will be the officers of the corporation, that is, president, vice president, secretary, and treasurer? It may be that the bylaws of the corporation should have a special description for specialized corporate officers. In very small corporations, there probably will not be this elaborate division of responsibilities and titles, but every corporation does need some officers.

☞ State statutes generally require a corporation to have some chief operating officer such as a president. In addition, state corporation laws may require administrative officers such as a secretary, and some state statutes require both.

Shareholders

How many shares should your corporation be authorized to issue? How many shares should be issued at the start of the corporation's business and how many held in reserve for future issuance? Should there be separate classes of shareholders? For example, some states permit the integration of professions within a single professional corporation. In these situations, you may wish to issue different classes of stock to the different types of professionals.

If the corporation is to be family owned, stock ownership may be used to some extent as a means of estate planning. You might, therefore, also wish to ask your attorney about updating your will at the same time you incorporate.

Shareholder Agreements

If your corporation has several shareholders, is there a method for preventing a shareholders' voting deadlock? You may also wish to discuss with your lawyer possible preincorporation shareholder agreements that govern employment status of key shareholders or commit shareholders to voting a certain way on specific corporate issues.

The Buy–Sell Agreement

The first meeting with your lawyer is a good time to discuss buy–sell agreements. What happens when one of the shareholders wishes to leave the business? Under what circumstances should he or she be able to sell to outsiders? Must the outsiders be licensed in the same profession as the selling shareholder? In closely held corporations, the corporation or other shareholders are generally granted the first option to buy the stock. What circumstances should trigger the corporation's or other shareholders' right to buy the stock—death, disability, retirement, termination, and so forth? Should the buy–sell agreement be tied to key-person insurance that would fund the purchase of stock by the corporation in the event of the death of a key shareholder? What will be the mechanism for valuing stock—annual appraisal, book value, multiple earnings, arbitration, or some other method?

Planning for Future Shareholders

Are there plans to take on additional practitioners in the future?

Capitalization

At this point, the attorney works closely with your CPA. What will the initial capitalization or funding of the corporation be? Will shareholders make loans to the corporation and contribute the rest in exchange for stock? What is being contributed by shareholders in exchange for stock—money, past services, equipment, assets of an ongoing business, licensing agreements, or other things? What value will be placed on assets that are contributed to the corporation?

The Board of Directors

Who will be on the board of directors? How many initial directors will there be? It is a good idea for there to be an odd number in order to avoid the potential for a voting deadlock. Will shareholders have the right to elect members of the board of directors based on their respective stock ownership?

Corporate Housekeeping

Your attorney will need to know several other details. For instance, the number of employees the corporation anticipates for the coming 12-month period must be stated on the application for a federal tax ID number. Will the corporation's accounting be on a cash basis or accrual basis? Will the corporation authorize salaries for its officers? What will be the date for the annual meeting of the board of directors and shareholders? Who will be the registered agent? Generally your attorney will assume this role.

Employee Benefits

Be prepared to consider employee benefit plans such as life and health insurance, profit sharing, pension or other retirement plans, stock option programs where possible, and other fringe benefits. If not implemented when the corporation is created, it is nonetheless a good idea to determine when such programs may be instituted.

Chapter S or Section C?

Will the corporation elect to be an S corporation, where income and losses flow directly to shareholders and the corporation pays no income tax, or will it be a standard so-called C corporation, where it does pay income tax and corporate income is not taxed to the shareholders? If the corporation is likely to sustain major losses and shareholders have other sources of income against which they wish to write off those losses, chances are the S election would be appropriate.

As you can see, there is much to discuss at the first meeting with your lawyer. A little time and thought prior to that meeting will prove to be a worthwhile investment.

3

Advertising

Advertising by health care professionals is a relatively new phenomenon. Both legal and ethical barriers have inhibited practitioners from developing advertising programs for their practices. Early on, professional associations themselves placed strict limitations on all forms of advertising and solicitation. Traditionally, this self-regulation was carried out through the promulgation of an ethical code, which strongly discouraged practitioners from advertising and soliciting patients. In addition, these admonitions were frequently also reflected in state licensure laws. These self-imposed restrictions were the result of concern over an increased likelihood of deception, which stemmed from the high degree of consumer dependence on health care professionals. In addition to this paternalistic motivation, most practitioners themselves simply viewed advertising as unprofessional and demeaning to the health care professions.

Today, many practitioners and professional associations still view advertising with skepticism and apprehension; however, several recent court decisions have significantly curtailed the ability of professional associations to prohibit their respective members from advertising.

Prior to 1975, the American Medical Association (AMA) essentially forbade any form of advertising or solicitation by its members. In that year, the Federal Trade Commission (FTC) challenged an AMA affiliate's advertising restrictions. While litigation was pending, the AMA issued a statement that evidenced a significant change in policy. Essentially, the statement declared that, while solicitation is still strictly forbidden, advertising was allowed under certain circumstances.

The FTC refused to drop its complaint, even though the AMA had signaled an intent to change its policy. In *In the Matter of the American Medical Association* (Docket No. 9064 (1982)), the FTC contended that the AMA affiliate's regulations restrained competition. The administrative law judge agreed with the FTC's position and ordered the AMA to cease and desist its illegal activities; however, the opinion was quite vague with respect to the restrictions that were still permissible.

In 1980, a federal court affirmed the FTC's ruling and clarified what restrictions were still permissible in *American Medical Association v. Federal Trade Commission*, 638 F.2d 443 (2d Cir. 1980). The court stated that the AMA could still "adopt guidelines . . . with respect to representations that the AMA reasonably believes to be false or deceptive." In other words, the AMA cannot prohibit advertising completely, but it can regulate advertising that is false or deceptive.

In 1982, the United States Supreme Court considered this issue; however, the Court was split 4 to 4. Accordingly, the lower court ruling was affirmed, but no opinion was written, and the consideration has no precedential value outside the Second Circuit. Still, given the fervor with which the FTC pursued the AMA in that earlier case, it is likely that the FTC would be just as inclined to pursue an AMA affiliate in another state that might try to regulate advertising other than "false or deceptive" advertising. In addition, although the ruling is directed specifically at the AMA, it is likely that a similar outcome would result from another professional association's attempt to restrict anything other than advertising that is false or deceptive.

Government Regulation

Representations about a product or service must be truthful and not likely to deceive the consumer. Although professional associations may restrict such advertising, the associations are limited to expulsion of the member from the association as a penalty for engaging in false or deceptive advertising.

Each state is in charge of regulating advertising within its own borders, through the state Attorney General's office. The Attorney General may file a lawsuit against business that engages in misleading advertising. Most states have consumer protection laws that, among other things, impose fines and other legal sanctions on businesses engaged in misleading advertising. The Attorney General can also cause an offending advertisement to be withdrawn. In addition, state licensure laws in some states regulate practitioner advertising. Violation of such a law may result in the revocation of the practitioner's license to practice in that particular state. Since the regulations vary from state to state, be sure to check your particular state's restrictions.

As noted earlier, the FTC is also involved in policing advertising; however, since the FTC is a federal agency, its jurisdiction is limited to businesses that are engaged in interstate commerce. That is to say, if your practice extends beyond your state boundaries and either touches or affects another state, then the FTC has jurisdiction over your practice.

Finally, there are special regulations pertaining to the development of a new product or service that may provide some medicinal benefits, such as a new type of therapy. Before you can advertise such a product or service, it must first be approved by the Food and Drug Administration (FDA). The approval process is quite technical and will require you to work closely with a lawyer specializing in this area of practice. Failure to comply with the requirements of the FDA could subject you to fines and, in some instances, imprisonment.

1. Problem Areas

False or misleading advertising is prohibited. Whether or not an advertisement is false is rather easy to evaluate—either the claim made can be substantiated or it cannot. Whether an advertisement is misleading or deceptive is more difficult to determine. The standard used is generally that of the ''reasonable patient''—would a reasonable patient be led to believe the particular claim?

Some forms of advertising are more likely to be deemed deceptive as a result of the subjective nature of the quality of services and great degree of variation in the quality of services from one practitioner to another. The following forms of advertising are those that tend to create a greater likelihood of deception and, therefore, should be used with care.

1. *Endorsements and Testimonials* Patient endorsements and testimonials are generally closely scrutinized. Since the quality of service received by one individual may vary greatly from the quality of service another receives, there is concern over the potential for deception. A testimonial that advocates a practitioner's services and expressly or implicitly communicates benefits that are not representative of the benefits an average patient would receive could raise unwarranted expectations about the practitioner's services. Such an advertisement would very likely be considered misleading or deceptive.

Several sources, including the FTC and several professional associations, have promulgated guidelines for the use of endorsements and testimonials. Those guidelines include the following:

1. The testimoniant's experience should reflect that of the "average patient." If the testimoniant's experience is not representative of the majority of patients, or there is a great degree of variance in the benefits that may be received, this should be made clear in the advertisement.

2. The testimonial should reflect the honest opinion and experience of the testimoniant, and should be made by an actual patient.

3. Although the testimonial need not be phrased in the exact words of the testimoniant, statements should not be taken out of context to imply a meaning that is different from the opinion of the testimoniant.

4. Testimoniants should not make objective claims concerning the safety, efficacy, benefits, or risks of a practitioner's services that cannot be soundly substantiated.

5. If an expert is used to endorse the practitioner's services, the expert's opinion should be based on an actual, independent evaluation of the practitioner's services that is at least as extensive as someone with the same degree of expertise would normally conduct.

Note: This list is not exhaustive and merely presents some minimum standards.

An issue related to the use of endorsements and testimonials is the use of photographs or models to portray the benefits that may be received through use of the practitioner's services. Where models are used in such a way as to suggest that the model received the practitioner's services, the ad should clearly state that the model is only a model and did not obtain the advertised services.

"Before-and-after" photographs are particularly susceptible to allegations of deceptive advertising. These photographs should both use the same lighting, poses, and techniques so that the "after" photo is not an unrealistic portrayal of the services rendered and benefits received. Advertising text accompanying the photographs should not misrepresent the actual healing time after the procedure. In addition, when a photograph represents results that are not representative of the results an average patient would receive, the advertisement should clearly disclose this fact.

2. *Comparative Advertising*   It is quite common for businesses of all kinds to boost the merits of their products and services by comparing them to those of their competitors. This form of advertising is permissible, provided that the statements made are true. Advertisements that compare the quality of services among several practitioners are dangerous. The quality of service given by varying practitioners is highly subjective and does not lend itself well to objective comparison. Consequently, there is a significant danger that such an advertisement may be construed as misleading.

Instead of comparing services, some practitioners simply compare fees and costs. Yet, if the fees are tied to services that vary greatly in quality, the problem of subjectivity (and the consequent propensity to mislead) arises once again. If you want to communicate your fee structure, the safer choice is to merely state your fees without making comparisons to other practitioners. Any claims you make regarding your fee structure should also indicate whether there are any collateral costs that are commonly associated with the advertised services.

A situation that occasionally arises in comparative advertising is when one makes disparaging remarks about the services of another. In this situation, the one who intentionally or (more commonly) negligently makes untrue, disparaging remarks about the services of another practitioner may be held legally accountable to the injured party. Thus, in a landmark case where a famous art critic stated that a particular painting was a forgery and the sale of that painting subsequently fell through, the critic was sued for the painting owner's lost profits. It should be noted that for a disparaging remark to be actionable, it must be both untrue and believed by a reasonable person. If the statement made was so outlandish as to be unbelievable, it is likely that the practitioner who was disparaged will not be able to prove any injury.

3. *Advertising an Area of Specialization* So long as you actually have the training, experience, and competence to practice the specialty advertised, statements that hold you out as a specialist in the field are highly unlikely to be construed as misleading.

II. Other Issues

1. *Publicity* Endorsements are frequently used, thus the appropriate rules deserve mention.

If a celebrity endorsement is used, it is necessary to first acquire the celebrity's consent. If not, you may be liable to the celebrity for violating his or her right of publicity. This right is granted to those who commercially exploit their names, voices, or images. In addition, the use of a lookalike for commercial purposes without an appropriate disclaimer may be actionable.

A person who has not achieved celebrity status is more likely to be used to endorse a practitioner's services. Even though such person is not well known, there is still a right of privacy, and thus a potential claim, if a noncelebrity's name or likeness is used in an advertisement without appropriate permission. If an individual's photograph, likeness, and so forth is not the focal point of the ad, but is merely an incidental part—such as a head in a crowd or a member of an audience—such individual's permission may not be essential before the photograph may be used in the ad. Even though you may not be required to obtain permission from the individual before using his or her photograph, it is a good idea to obtain a signed photo release whenever possible. The release should be worded in such a way as to give your business permission to use the name, likeness, or voice for any and all purposes, including advertising your practice.

2. *Trademark* An advertiser may be permitted to use the trademark of another business in an ad so long as there is no likelihood that the average reader would believe the ad was sponsored by the company whose trademark is being used. In other words, so long as there is

no likelihood of confusion between your services and the trademark belonging to another, you may use the other's trademark. Thus it may be permissible for you to have an ad for your services contain a photo of an individual holding a distinctively shaped Coca-Cola bottle (which is a federally registered trademark), so long as it is clear from the advertisement that the Coca-Cola Company is not the source of your services and so long as you do not disparage Coca-Cola.

3. *Geographic Locations*   Geographic locations may also be used in advertisements without obtaining the owner's consent. It would be permissible for a practice to advertise its services by having someone stand in front of the Empire State Building. Since items of utility are not copyrightable, buildings, parks, and other landmarks are not protectable under the copyright laws and may be used in advertising programs without their owners' permission. One cautionary note, though—standing in front of a well-known hospital or treatment center creates the possibility of confusion. If your practice is not affiliated with such a facility, this should be made explicitly clear in the advertisement.

4. *Copyright*   Advertisements, flyers, booklets, and any textual material written or commissioned by you may be entitled to copyright protection. In fact, any original work of authorship that is put in some tangible form will likely enjoy the benefits of the federal copyright law. While copyright protection is automatic, it is a good idea to use a copyright notice: ©, copyright; your name; and the year in which the work was first distributed to the public. In addition, if you register the work with the Copyright Office, you will be entitled to several significant remedies if someone copies your protected material without your permission. Registration is quite simple and merely requires you to deposit two copies of the work, complete the appropriate registration form (TX in the case of textual material), and pay a $20 fee. An intellectual property attorney can assist you in identifying your copyrightable material and registering it.

Advertising within the health care industry remains less prevalent than in other areas of professional services. If you should choose to advertise, it is essential that your advertisements be truthful and not misrepresent the costs, efficacy, and benefits of your services. In addition, you must be careful not to violate the rights of other businesses or individuals and to protect your own. Care should be taken to work with an attorney skilled in advertising law in order to be assured of having an effective program that will enable you to promote your services without exposing yourself to liability. A poorly drafted advertising program is likely to be more harmful than none at all.

4

People Who Work for You

There comes a time in the life of almost every medical practice when it is necessary to get help, be it brain or brawn. The help most commonly needed first is the bookkeeper/receptionist, who can handle patients, phones, billing, and the like. When things get a little hectic around the office, you might then hire someone to help with patient control, such as a nurse or medical assistant. As your practice grows, you may soon have to hire more employees such as, for example, a full-time lab technician, to keep up with increased demands.

Independent Contractors

Someone hired on a one-time or job-by-job basis is called an *independent contractor*. Although paid for their services by the hiring firm or individual, contractors remain their own bosses and may even employ others to actually do the work.

If once or twice a year you hire an accountant to prepare your financial statements and tax returns, that person is an independent contractor. The fact that the person is independent, and not your employee, means that you do not have to pay Social Security, withhold income taxes, obtain a workers' compensation policy, or comply with the myriad of rules imposed on employers.

More important, you are generally not liable for injuries to a third party resulting from the independent contractor's negligence or wrongful acts, even while working for you. However, there are situations where, despite your innocence, an independent contractor can render you legally responsible for his or her wrongful acts. Such situations fall into three basic categories:

- If an employer is careless in hiring an independent contractor and a careful investigation would have disclosed facts to indicate that the contractor was not qualified, the employer may be liable when the independent contractor fails to properly perform the job.
- If a job is so dangerous as to be characterized as "ultrahazardous" (a legal term) and is to be performed for the employer's benefit, then, regardless of who performs the work, the employer will remain legally responsible for any injuries that occur during the performance of the work. For example, a medical professional cannot escape liability by using an X-ray technician who is an independent contractor.
- An employer may be required by law to perform certain tasks for the health and safety of the community.

These responsibilities are said to be nondelegable—that is, an employer cannot delegate them and thus escape liability for their improper performance. If, therefore, a nondelegable duty is performed by an independent contractor, the employer will remain responsible for any injury that results. A good example of a nondelegable duty is the law (common in many states) that propety owners are responsible for keeping their sidewalks free of dangerous obstacles. If a physician hires an independent contractor to fulfill this obligation by removing ice during the winter, the physician is still legally liable if someone is injured on the slippery sidewalk, even if the accident resulted from the contractor's carelessness.

Employees

The second capacity in which someone can work for you is as an *employee*. This category includes anyone over whose work you exercise direct control—nurses, receptionists, and bookkeepers, all of whom are full-time members of your staff, and so forth. The formation of this relationship entails nothing more than an agreement on your side to hire someone and an agreement by that person to work. Although a written contract is not necessary for enforcement except in the case of employment for more than one year, I suggest that employment terms be put down in writing so that there is no misunderstanding later.

Employment Contracts

If the employment is to be for more than one year, there must be a written contract specifying the period of employment; otherwise, either party may terminate the relationship at any time. While there is no prescribed form that the contract must take, there are nevertheless certain items that should be considered. The first item of an employment contract is the term of employment. An employment contract may be either terminable at will or for a fixed duration. Making the contract for a fixed period gives the employee some job security and creates a moral and contractual obligation for the employee to remain for the term. Of course, if the employee chooses to quit, or the employer chooses to fire the employee, the law will not compel fulfillment of the contract. That went out with selling orphans into apprenticeships and other forms of slavery.

The second item is the wage. Unless you are a large employer with 45 or more employees, or are engaged in interstate commerce (which is defined as having gross sales of $500,000 or more), you will not have to comply with federal minimum-wage laws, but most states have their own minimum-wage laws. Above the requirement imposed by this law, the amount of remuneration is open to bargaining.

In addition to an hourly wage or monthly salary, other benefits can be given, such as health and life insurance or retirement pensions. The cost of professional liability insurance may also be paid by the employer. If this is the case, the employment contract should specify which party will purchase post-employment, or "tail," coverage at the termination of employment. If it is not specified, then there is case law holding that the employer is required to purchase insurance. Some legal advice may be necessary here in order to take advantage of tax laws. In the event no salary is specified, the law will presume a reasonable wage for the work performed. Thus you cannot escape paying your employees fairly by not discussing the amount they will earn. If you hire a nurse and the accepted salary in your region for a qualified nurse is $30 per hour, it will be presumed that the nurse was hired for this amount unless you and that person have agreed to a different salary.

Third, it is often wise to spell out your employee's duties in the employment contract. This serves as a form of orientation for the employee and also may limit future conflicts over what is and what is not involved in the job.

Fourth, you may want your employee to agree not to work for someone else while working for you or, more importantly, not to compete against you at the end of the employment period. The latter agreement must be carefully drawn to be enforceable. Such an agreement must not be overly broad in the kind of work the employee may not do; it must cover a geographic area no broader than that in which you actually operate; and it must be for a reasonable duration— a five-year period has been upheld. Thus, if you hire a young associate to assist you with your practice, it is a good idea to have your attorney draft a noncompete agreement prior to the commencement of this relationship that is no broader than necessary to protect your practice. Some medical associations appear to frown on the use of restrictive covenants. You should therefore contact your local medical association to determine its position on this situation.

Finally, grounds for termination of the employment contract should be listed. Even if the contract is terminable at will, these grounds serve as useful benchmarks to guide your employee's actions.

Unlike the situation where you have hired an independent contractor, you are "vicariously liable" for the negligence and, sometimes, even the intentional wrongdoing of your employee when the employee is acting on your behalf. That means that if your employee is on the job and is involved in an automobile accident that is his or her fault, you as well as your employee are legally liable. It would be wise to be extremely careful when hiring, and to contact your insurance agent to obtain sufficient insurance coverage for your additional exposure.

Other Considerations in Hiring

There are other issues you should consider when hiring an employee, many of which fall into the realm of accounting or bookkeeping responsibilities. You should, therefore, consult with your accountant or bookkeeper regarding items such as the following:

1. A workers' compensation policy for your employees in the event of on-the-job injury or occupational illness. State laws vary on the minimum number of employees that triggers this very important requirement. Many states' workers' compensation laws provide that an employer who has failed to obtain or keep in force required workers' compensation insurance will be strictly liable, even in the absence of negligence, for on-the-job injury or illness, including not only medical expenses but also damages for pain and suffering, lost earning potential, and other damages that are a consequence of injuries.

2. Withholding taxes: federal, state, and local. Here, too, the laws vary, and you must find out what is required in your locale.

3. Social Security (FICA). There are some exemptions from this body of social legislation. Contact your nearby Social Security office to determine how these exemptions may affect you.

4. Unemployment insurance, both federal and state. These also include certain technical requirements for subcontractors and the like.

5. Health and safety regulations, both federal and state.

6. Municipal taxes for specific programs such as schools or public transportation.

7. Employee benefits such as insurance coverage (medical, dental, legal), retirement benefits, memberships, parking, and so on.

8. Union requirements if your employees are subject to union contracts.

9. Wage and hour laws, both federal and state. These include minimum wage and overtime requirements. In some states, the law also regulates holidays and vacations, as well as the method of paying employees during employment and upon termination.

In addition, there are federal and state prohibitions against discrimination in hiring, promotion, and termination. This area is quite complex and you should consult your attorney before establishing any employment policies and procedures. You are federally prohibited from discriminating on the basis of race, creed, sex, age, national origin, disability, or religion. There may be additional state or local restrictions.

As already noted, the requirements of these laws may vary dramatically from state to state, and you are well advised to discuss them with your lawyer, accountant, and bookkeeper. In addition, you should find out whether any other forms of employment legislation, such as licensing requirements, apply to you, your employees, or your business.

Hazards in the Workplace

On February 10, 1983, a 61-year-old Polish-born employee of a film-recovery company in Chicago died of cyanide poisoning. He had worked for a small company that extracted silver from X-ray and photographic film. The work force consisted primarily of Polish and Mexican-American employees who spoke little English and were not very sophisticated. Many of the employees were not in this country legally.

To extract the silver, the film-recovery workers put the film in a vat containing cyanide and then transferred the film to a second vat, which extracted the silver. The work was labor-intensive and the vats were not properly vented and emitted dangerous fumes. Many of the employees complained of symptoms associated with cyanide poisoning, such as dizziness, nausea, and a bitter taste in the mouth. The employer made no efforts to warn them of the hazards of the work.

After the employee died and was examined by a county medical officer, it was determined that the cause of death was cyanide poisoning. Government officials examined the plant where the employee had worked and found numerous health and safety violations. Eight months later, the president of the company and numerous corporate officials, as well as the company itself, were charged with and convicted of murder. The court concluded that the company, its officers, and directors were aware of the serious risk and hazards resulting from cyanide use, but they took no steps to alleviate the hazards in the plant. They did not even post warning signs that the foreign-born employees could understand.

While few medical professionals would intentionally injure a fellow human being, you may nevertheless find yourself in a similar situation. It is not uncommon to use hazardous materials or be exposed to dangerous substances in a medical or dental practice. Often employees are not aware of the potential hazard that may result from such exposure. It is advisable to research the potentially dangerous nature of all substances used in your practice, whether they are labeled for toxicity or not. You must then disclose to your employees at hiring any pertinent information regarding hazardous substances. This is particularly true today, with the prevalence of the HIV virus at all levels of society. With respect to blood-borne diseases in particular, the law requires employers to establish a fairly rigorous safety program. The program must include, among other things, education and acquiring equipment, and in addition there are certain optional procedures. The employer must also keep accurate records of the employee's physical condition in order to determine whether the employee has contracted any blood-related diseases. If an employment contract is used, a paragraph containing such a disclosure and the employee's acknowledgment of the known risks should be incorporated in the contract. A similar statement should also be included in any employment handbook.

While these documents would not provide a defense to a workers' compensation claim, they would sensitize employees to the need for caution in working with hazardous substances. Needless to say, you must take all precautions possible to protect the health and safety of your employees.

Congress and federal administrative agencies are becoming more active in the field of regulation of hazardous substances. You should also be aware that your state workers' compensation agency or the Occupational Safety and Health Administration may have passed special rules regarding specific workplace substances and activities. It is critical to obtain a lawyer's opinion as to whether any of these regulations apply to your practice. Your state's Labor Department may also be able to give you information regarding applicable workplace regulations.

Termination of Employment

Determining whether someone is an employee or an independent contractor is not always easy. The reason that the characterization is important is that employers are responsible for employees' income tax withholding, Social Security, workers' compensation and the like, whereas employers who hire independent contractors are not.

There is another reason that the characterization may be important. If the individual working for you is an independent contractor, the contract between you and that person will govern your respective rights of termination. On the other hand, if the individual is an employee, care must be taken not to become responsible for a wrongful termination when dismissing the individual.

Historically, an employee who was not under contract could be terminated for any reason whatsoever. Approximately 25 years ago, this right of absolute dismissal was challenged and the rule was modified. At that time, it was held that an employee could be terminated for the right reason or for no reason at all, but could not be terminated for the wrong reason. Thus an employee who was terminated for refusing to commit perjury before a legislative committee was entitled to recover against the employer for wrongful termination. The public policy in having individuals testify honestly was considered more important than the employer's right to control the employment relationship.

Recently, courts have become even more protective of the rights of employees. Thus, in a 1983 case, *Novosel v. Nationwide Insurance Company*, the United States Circuit Court of Appeals held that the power to hire and fire could not be used to dictate an employee's political activity, and that even a nongovernment entity is limited by the Constitution in its power to discharge an employee. The court, in essence, held that one's right to exercise constitutionally protected free speech was more important than the employer's right to control an employee's conduct.

Wrongful termination cases fall into three general categories. These include firing someone for (1) refusing to commit an unlawful act, such as committing perjury or refusing to participate in welfare or Medicare fraud; (2) performing a public obligation, such as serving on a jury or serving in a military reserve unit; and (3) exercising a statutory right, such as filing a claim for workers' compensation. Employers may not legally terminate an employee for the foregoing reasons. In an amusing case, the Arizona Supreme Court held that a nurse who was terminated for refusing to "moon" fellow employees in a parody of the song "Moon River" during a hospital staff retreat was entitled to damage for wrongful termination. The public policy of protecting her right of privacy was deemed more important than the employer's right to terminate employees for disobedience. The courts appear to go quite far in holding that an employer cannot discharge an employee unless there is just cause for termination. A number of states have considered the adoption of legislation that would restrict the employer's right to terminate an employee to cases in which there was just cause. These laws also contain specific prohibitions on the termination of employees for "whistleblowing," that is, cases in which employees notify government authorities of wrongful acts by the employer, such as tax evasion, or cases in which employees tell licensing boards about wrongful acts of medical practitioners.

Employers should take some precautions to avoid being placed in the untenable position of having bound themselves to individuals in their employment when the relationship has soured. This can result from language in employee handbooks that might be construed as giving rise to a contractual right. It is also possible that oral statements made by recruiters or interviewers could give rise to contractual rights. To avoid this problem, an employer should have a legend placed in any employee handbook making it clear that the material is not an employment contract. It has also become common for employers to require prospective employees to sign a statement making it clear that the employment is "at will" and does not give rise to any contractual right. If there is a probationary period, the employer should be careful to state that the probationary employee will become a "regular" or "full-time" employee rather than a "permanent" employee. In addition, if there is any evaluation of the employee after the probationary period has ended, it should be conducted fairly. When evaluations become merely pro forma, problems can and do arise. Employees may argue that they have received sparkling evaluations and are being terminated for some invalid reason.

Perhaps an employer who uses evaluations should employ what has been characterized as progressive discipline. This procedure would be to start by orally warning a problem employee of your concern and progressively imposing disciplinary practices until termination becomes the only form of recourse left. Care should be taken not to violate the employee's rights since the liability for wrongful termination can be catastrophic to a medical practice. When in doubt, an employer should contact an attorney with some experience in the field of employment relations. In this area, as with many others, preproblem counseling can prevent a good deal of time-consuming and costly litigation.

5

Contracts

Contracts constitute a fundamental legal and practical problem in virtually every business, including medical, dental, and other health care practices. Clearly, we cannot cover the entire field of contract law, but perhaps I can help you become aware of some of the ramifications of contract law and enable you to see where you need protection.

What Is a Contract?

A contract is a legally binding promise or set of promises. The law requires that the parties to a contract perform the promises they have made to each other. In the event of nonperformance—usually called a *breach*—the law provides remedies to the injured party. For the purposes of this discussion, we will assume that the contract is between two people, though it can involve business organizations such as partnerships or professional corporations as well.

The three basic elements of every contract are the *offer*, the *acceptance*, and the *consideration*. For example, suppose a salesperson shows a doctor a Mustang convertible at an automobile lot and suggests that she buy it (the offer). The doctor says she likes it and wants it (the acceptance). They agree on a price (the consideration).

That is the basic framework, but a great many variations can be played on that theme.

Types of Contracts

Contracts may be *express* or *implied*; they may be *oral* or *written*. On this latter point, there are at least two types of contracts that must be in writing if they are to be legally enforceable: (1) any contract that, by its terms, cannot be completed in less than one year, and (2) any contract that involves the sale of goods for over $500.

An express contract is one in which all the details are spelled out. For example, you might make a contract with a pharmaceutical company for a specific quantity of flu vaccine to be delivered to you on October 1, at a specific price, to be paid for within 30 days of receipt.

That is fairly straightforward. If either party fails to live up to any material part of the contract, a breach has occurred, and the other party may withhold performance of his or her obligation until receiving assurance that the breaching party will perform. In the event no such assurance is forthcoming, the aggrieved party may have a cause of action and go to court for breach of contract.

If the serum is delivered on October 15 and you had scheduled a flu vaccine clinic during the week of October 1, and had notified the supplier of that fact, time was an important consideration and you would not be required to accept the late shipment. But if time is not a material consideration, then even with the slight delay this probably would be considered "substantial performance" and you would have to accept the delivery.

Express contracts can be either oral or written, though if you are going to the trouble of expressing contractual terms you should put your understanding in writing.

Implied contracts need not be very complicated, either, though they are usually not done in writing. An example might be if you call a supplier to order tongue depressors without making any express statement that you will pay for them. The promise to pay is implied in the order, and is enforceable when the product is delivered.

But with implied contracts, things can often become a lot stickier. Suppose your staff neglects to obtain a new patient's signature on the appropriate form obligating the patient to pay for services. You fill the patient's cavity.

Is there an implied contract to pay in this arrangement? That may depend on whether you are normally in the business of giving away your services.

You enter into many contracts without thinking much about them, such as those exchanges of promises that take place between your business and the company supplying your telephone service. (The telephone company agrees to provide certain telecommunications services in exchange for your promise to pay for those services under certain agreed-upon terms.)

Perhaps the more problematic contracts are those that you enter into on a regular but intermittent basis for the purchase or sale of goods and services critical to the ongoing viability and smooth running of your practice.

Let us examine the principles of offer, acceptance, and consideration in the context of several potential situations for a hypothetical business owner, Pat Smith.

Smith is an automobile dealer who has an impressive collection of vintage cars restored to mint condition. We will look at the following situations and see whether an enforceable contract comes into existence.

At a cocktail party, Dr. Jones expresses an interest in Smith's cars. "It looks like the market value of your cars keeps going up," Dr. Jones tells Smith. "I'm going to buy one while I can still afford it."

Is this a contract? If so, what are the terms of the offer—the particular car, the specific price? No, this is not really an offer that Smith can accept. It is nothing more than an opinion or a vague expression of intent.

Brown offers to pay $4000 for one of Smith's cars that she saw in an auto show several weeks ago. At the show, it was listed at $4500, but Smith agrees to accept the lower price.

Is this an enforceable contract? Yes! Brown has offered, in unambiguous terms, to pay a specific amount for a specific car, and Smith has accepted the offer. A binding contract exists.

One day Dr. Jones shows up at Smith's vintage-auto lot and sees a particular car for which he offers $4500. Smith accepts and promises to transfer title the next week, at which time Dr. Jones will pay for it. An hour later, Dr. Brown shows up. She likes the same car and offers Smith $6000 for it. Can Smith accept the later offer?

No—a contract exists with Dr. Jones. An offer was made and accepted. The fact that the object has not yet been delivered or paid for does not make the contract any less binding.

Dr. Green discusses certain renovations he would like Smith to perform on a particular car Smith has just acquired. He offers to pay $6000 for the car if the final product is satisfactory to him. Dr. Green approves preliminary sketches, and Smith completes the work. But when Dr. Green shows up to pick up his car, he refuses to accept it because it does not satisfy him.

Dr. Green is making the offer in this case, but the offer is conditional upon his satisfaction with the completed work. Smith can only accept the offer by producing something that meets Dr. Green's subjective standards—a risky business. There is no enforceable contract for payment until such time as Dr. Green indicates that the completed work is satisfactory.

Suppose Dr. Green comes to Smith's vintage-car lot and says that the car is satisfactory but then, when Smith delivers it, says he has changed his mind. That is too late. The contract became binding at the moment he indicated the work to be satisfactory. If he then refuses to accept it, he would be breaching his contract.

Earlier I mentioned that contracts for goods over $500 must be in writing. The last example described was of a hybrid sale, for goods and services. Since the goods involved were over $500 in value, the contract should be in writing to ensure enforceability. However, if the contract had been one for performance of personal services only— say, for renovation to be performed by Smith on Dr. Green's own car or for your medical services—the Uniform Commercial Code (UCC) would not apply and the contract would be enforceable whether it was reduced to writing or not. (The UCC is a compilation of commercial laws enacted in every state except Louisiana.)

Oral or Written Contracts?

Contracts are enforceable only if they can be proven. All of the hypothetical examples mentioned above could have been oral contracts, but a great deal of detail is often lost in the course of remembering a conversation. The best practice, of course, is to get it in writing. The function of a written contract is not only that of proof but also to make very clear the understanding of the parties regarding the agreement and the terms of the contract.

Some medical practitioners prefer to do business strictly on the basis of so-called "gentlemen's agreements," particularly with their immediate suppliers and retailers. The assumption seems to be that the best business relations are those based on mutual trust alone.

Although there may be some validity to this, medical practitioners nevertheless really should put all oral agreements into writing. Far too many trusting people have suffered adverse consequences because of their idealistic reliance on the sanctity of oral contracts.

Under even the best of business relationships, it is still possible that one or both parties might forget the terms of an oral agreement. Or both parties might have quite different perceptions about the precise terms of the agreement reached. When, however, the agreement is put into writing, there is much less doubt as to the terms of the arrangement, although even a written contract may contain ambiguities if it is not drafted with considerable care. Thus a written contract generally functions as a safeguard against subsequent misunderstanding or forgetful minds.

Perhaps the principal problem with oral contracts lies in the fact that they cannot always be proven or enforced.

Proof of oral contracts typically centers around the conflicting testimony of the parties involved. And if one of the parties is not able to establish by a preponderance of evidence that his or her version of the contract is the correct one, the oral contract may be considered nonexistent—as though it had never been made. The same result might ensue if the parties cannot remember the precise terms of the agreement, and memories do fade.

When Written Contracts Are Necessary

Even if an oral contract is established, it may not always be enforceable. As already noted, there are some agreements that must be in writing in order to be legally enforceable.

An early law that was designed to prevent fraud and perjury, known as the Statute of Frauds, provides that any contract that by its terms cannot be fully performed within one year must be in writing. This rule is narrowly interpreted, so if there is *any* possibility, no matter how remote, that the contract *could* be fully performed within one year, the contract need not be reduced to writing.

For example, if a physician agreed to provide physical exams to employees of a local business each year for a period of five years, the contract would have to be in writing since by the very terms of the agreement there is no way the contract could be performed within one year. If, on the other hand, the contract called for the physician to perform five physicals within a period of five years, the contract would not have to be in writing under the Statute of Frauds, since it is possible, though perhaps not probable, that the physician would perform all five physicals within the first year. The fact that the doctor does not actually complete performance of the contract within one year is immaterial. So long as complete performance within one year is within the realm of possibility, the contract need not be in writing to be enforceable; it may be oral.

The Statute of Frauds further provides that any contract for the sale of goods valued at $500 or more is not enforceable unless it has been put into writing and signed by the party against whom enforcement is being sought. The fact that a contract for a price in excess of $500 is not in writing does not void the agreement or render it illegal. The parties are free to perform the oral arrangement, but, if one party refuses to perform, the other will be unable to legally enforce the agreement.

The law defines *goods* as all things that are movable at the time of making the contract except for the money used as payment. The real question becomes whether a particular contract involves the sale of goods for a price of $500 or more. Although the answer would generally seem to be fairly clear, ambiguities may arise.

For example, if a supplier agrees to provide a practice with all its pharmaceutical needs for the coming year, how is the price to be determined? Or if the pharmaceutical company sells a variety of items to a doctor where the total purchase price exceeds $500 but the price of an individual item is less than $500, which price governs? In light of these possible ambiguities the safest course is to put all oral contracts into writing.

No-Cost Written Agreements

At this point, medical practitioners might object, asserting that they do not have the time, energy, or patience to draft contracts. After all, they are in business to provide a service, not to formulate written contracts steeped in legal jargon.

Fortunately, the medical practitioner will not always be required to do this, since the supplier will generally have a satisfactory contract in the form of an invoice. However, be wary of signing any form contracts; *they will almost invariably be one-sided*, with all terms in favor of whoever paid to have them drafted.

As an alternative, the medical practitioner could employ an attorney to draft contracts. But this might be worthwhile only for substantial transactions; for example, contracts for the purchase or sale of a practice, including a sale to a hospital; similarly, contracts with third-party payors such as insurance companies. In these situations you should retain an attorney experienced in health law. With respect to smaller transactions, the legal fees may be much larger than the benefits derived from having a written contract.

The Uniform Commercial Code provides businesses with a third and perhaps the best alternative. Businesses need not draft contracts or rely on anyone else (a supplier, retailer, or attorney) to do so.

The UCC provides that where both parties are merchants and one party sends to the other a written confirmation of an oral contract within a reasonable time after that contract was made, and the recipient does not object to the confirming memorandum within ten days of its receipt, the contract will be deemed enforceable.

A *merchant* is defined as any person who normally deals in goods of the kind sold or who because of occupation represents herself or himself as having knowledge or skill peculiar to the practices or goods involved in the transaction.

It should be emphasized that the sole effect of the confirming memorandum is that neither party can use the Statute of Frauds as a defense, assuming that the recipient fails to object within ten days after receipt. The party sending the confirming memorandum must still prove that an oral contract was, in fact, made prior to or at the same time as the written confirmation. But once such proof is established, neither party can raise the Statute of Frauds to avoid enforcement of agreement.

The advantage of the confirming memorandum over a written contract lies in the fact that the confirming memorandum can be used without the active participation of the other contracting party. It would suffice, for example, to simply state ''This memorandum is to confirm our oral agreement.''

But since you would still have to prove the terms of that agreement, it would be useful to provide a bit more detail in the confirming memorandum, such as the subject of the contract, the date it was made, and the price or other consideration to be paid. Thus you might draft something like the following:

> This memorandum is to confirm our oral agreement made on July 3, 1991, pursuant to which supplier agreed to deliver to purchaser on or before September 19, 1991, five thousand sheets of letterhead for the purchase price of $600.

The advantages of providing some detail in the confirming memorandum are twofold. First, in the event of a dispute, you could introduce the memorandum as proof of the terms of the oral agreement. And second, the recipient of the memorandum will be precluded from offering any proof regarding the terms of the oral contract that contradicts the terms contained in the memorandum. The recipient or, for that matter, the party sending the memorandum can introduce proof only regarding the terms of the oral contract that are consistent with the terms, if any, found in the memorandum. Thus the purchaser in the above example would be precluded from claiming that the contract called for delivery of ten thousand sheets of letterhead because the quantity was stated in the written memo and not objected to.

On the other hand, the purchaser would be permitted to testify that the oral contract required the supplier to use high-quality rag paper since this testimony would not be inconsistent with the terms stated in the memorandum.

One party to a contract can prevent the other from adding or inventing terms that are not spelled out in the confirming memorandum by ending the memorandum with a clause requiring all other provisions to be contained in a written and signed document. Such a clause might read:

This is the entire agreement between the parties and no modification, alteration, or additional terms shall be enforceable unless in writing and signed by both parties.

To sum up, doctors, dentists, and other licensed medical professionals should not rely on oral contracts alone since they offer little protection in the event of a dispute. The best protection is afforded by a written contract. It is a truism that oral contracts are not worth the paper they are written on. If drafting a complete written contract proves too burdensome or too costly, the medical practitioner should at least submit a memorandum in confirmation of the oral contract. That at least surpasses the initial barrier raised by the Statute of Frauds. Moreover, by recounting the terms in the memorandum, the medical practitioner is in a much better position to prove the oral contract.

Summary of Essentials to Put in Writing

A contract rarely need be—or should be—a long, complicated document written in legal jargon designed to provide a handsome income to lawyers. Indeed, a contract should be written in simple language that both parties can understand, and should spell out the terms of the agreement.

The contract would include (1) the date of the agreement; (2) identification of the two parties, the buyer and seller in the case of sale of goods or services; (3) a description of the goods or services sold; (4) price or other consideration; and (5) the signatures of the parties involved.

To supplement these basics, the agreement should spell out whatever other terms might be applicable: pricing arrangements, payment schedules, insurance coverage, consignment details, and so forth.

Finally, it should be noted that a written document that leaves out essential terms of the contract presents many of the same problems of proof and ambiguity as an oral contract. Contract terms should be well conceived, clearly drafted, conspicuous (i.e., not in tiny print that no one can read), and in plain English so everyone understands what the terms of the contract are.

6

Borrowing from Banks

Commercial loans can be a valuable source of needed capital for medical professionals who need additional financing.

Lending policies vary dramatically from institution to institution. You should, therefore, talk to several banks to determine which might be likely to lend to your business and which have the most favorable loan terms. While lenders by nature are conservative in their lending policies, you may discover some to be more flexible than others. To save time and increase the chances of loan approval, it makes sense to approach first those banks that are most likely to view your proposal favorably, and whose lending criteria you feel you can meet.

Your search for a loan should not be limited to your community. A statewide, regional, or even national search may be necessary before you find the right combination of willing lender and favorable terms.

Having shopped the marketplace and decided on a particular bank, you will be ready for the next step: preparing the loan proposal. The importance of being properly prepared before taking this critical step cannot be overemphasized. Loan officers are not likely to be impressed by a hastily prepared application containing vague, incomplete information and unsubstantiated claims. Many loan requests are doomed at this early stage because ill-prepared applicants fail to adequately present themselves and their practice to the lender, even though the proposed ventures are in fact sound. What, then, should a borrower understand about the lending process?

The Loan Proposal

Inexperience with the bank's lending procedures can result in an unexpected rejection. Knowing the bank's lending policy and following its procedure is, therefore, essential. Just what does a lender look for in a loan application? At a minimum, a borrower should be prepared to satisfactorily address each of the following questions:

1. Is your practice creditworthy?
2. Do you need a short-term (one year or less) or long-term (more than one year) loan? For what purpose?
3. How much money do you really need?
4. What kind of collateral do you and your practice have to secure the loan?
5. What are the lender's rules, and what limitations would apply to this loan?

The lender's decision to grant or refuse the loan request will be based on your answers to these questions.

Is Your Practice Creditworthy?

The ability to obtain money when you need it may be as important to the operation of your practice as having a good location and the right equipment. But before an institution will agree to lend you money, the loan officer must be satisfied that you and your business constitute a good risk—that is, that you are creditworthy. This decision will include several considerations.

Do You Have a Good Reputation?

The lender will want to know what sort of person you are. Do you have a good reputation in the community and in your profession? Are you known in the community? What is your past credit history, and what is the likelihood that you will repay the loan if your practice falters or even fails?

Despite its subjective nature, this character factor figures prominently in the lender's decision making. It is not uncommon for a loan officer to deny a loan request, regardless of how qualified the applicant appears on paper, if the officer is not convinced of the borrower's good character. Even for "signature loans"—those that require only the applicant's signature, available only to those with the highest credit standing, business integrity, and management skills—the applicant's character will affect the institution's decision to make a loan, even when well collateralized.

For What Is the Money Needed?

Is the money needed to cover a cash flow problem or to acquire fixed assets, such as medical equipment? The answer to this will determine what type of loan—long-term or short-term—the applicant should request. Loans needed to cover a cash flow problem will generally be short-term loans, requiring repayment within one year or less. This is because the bank will likely anticipate repayment from the collection of your accounts receivable.

Intermediate-term loans, requiring payment between one and five years, and long-term loans, which are those extending payments over ten or even fifteen years, are more appropriate for purchases of fixed assets, since repayment is expected to be made not from the sale of these assets but from the earnings generated by your ongoing use of them. Those assets produce income at a much slower rate, hence the bank's willingness to allow repayment over a longer period. Bear in mind that commercial lenders are interested in offering funds to successful businesses in need of additional capital to expand and increase profitability. They are not as inclined to make loans to businesses needing the money to pay off existing debts.

When and How Will the Loan Be Repaid?

When and how the loan will be repaid is closely associated with the preceding questions of how much money is needed and for what purpose. The banker will now use judgment and professional experience to assess your business ability and the likelihood of your future success. The banker will want to know whether the proposed use of the borrowed funds justifies the repayment schedule requested. You as the borrower must be able to demonstrate that the cash flow anticipated from the proceeds of the loan will be adequate to meet the repayment terms if the loan is granted.

Is the Cushion on the Loan Large Enough?

The lender will want to know if the borrower has included in the loan request a suitable allowance for unexpected developments. That is, does the loan proposal realistically allow for the vicissitudes of operating a medical practice and provide for alternative resources to meet the borrower's obligation if the business expectations are not met? Or is the borrower stretching to the limit, leaving no margin for error, so that repayment can be made only if the proposal is successful? In the latter circumstance, the lender may consider the loan too risky.

The Business Outlook

The lender will be evaluating the business outlook for your practice in particular, and for your type of practice in general, in light of contemporary economic realities. Can your proposed use of the loan be reasonably expected to produce the anticipated increased revenues for your practice? While your proposed plan may appear viable on paper, it may not be realistic given the state of the economy within which you operate.

Financial Evidence

Remember that bankers prefer to make loans to solvent, profitable, growing ventures. They seek assurance that the loan will contribute to that growth since your repayment ability is directly related to your success. As noted previously, bankers are not interested in lending money so that a practice can pay off already existing loans. To aid the bank in understanding the financial health of your practice, you probably will be asked to provide specific financial data. Two basic financial documents are customarily submitted for this purpose: the balance sheet and the profit and loss statement. The balance sheet will aid the bank in evaluating your practice's solvency, while the profit and loss statement summarizes its current performance. Unless yours is a new practice, you should be prepared to submit these financial reports for at least the past two or three years, since they are the principal means for measuring your stability and growth potential. Ideally, these statements will have been prepared by an independent Certified Public Accountant (CPA).

Analyzing Your Practice's Potential

In interviewing loan applicants and in studying the financial records of their businesses, the bank is especially interested in the following facts and figures.

General Information

Are the books and financial records up to date, accurate, and in good condition, or are they incomplete, infrequently maintained, and in disarray? Haphazard recordkeeping not only fails to reflect the true financial state but also demonstrates poor managerial skills. For obvious reasons, banks are reluctant to back poorly run businesses, viewing them as too risky.

The lender will also be interested in the current condition of your accounts payable and notes payable. Are those obligations being paid in a timely fashion, or are they overdue? If you are not presently able to meet existing debts, the lender will be hard-pressed to understand how you expect to be able to meet any additional obligations. Perhaps the requested funds will solve cash-flow problems you now have and will also increase earnings so that you will be able to bring past-due accounts current while adequately handling the added debt. In this situation, you might overcome the lender's skepticism by presenting a well-thought-out, solid business plan that clearly demonstrates how the new loan will solve, rather than add to, the practice's financial problems and will boost revenues.

Additionally, the lender will likely want to know your salary as well as other employees' salaries to see if they are reasonable. Excessive salaries represent an unacceptable drain on the practice's resources and profits, which may adversely affect the ability to meet debt obligations.

The lender will also be interested in the size of your work force. Does it seem adequate to maximize the practice's potential, or does it seem excessive compared to other, similar practices?

You should be prepared to discuss the adequacy of your insurance coverage and your present tax situation (whether all taxes are current).

All of these factors say something about the financial state of your practice. Although the lender may inquire into other areas, the borrower who knows the type of general information of interest to a lender, and who can present this information articulately, significantly increases the chances of having the loan approved.

Accounts Receivable

Of particular interest to the bank will be the number of patients that are behind in their payments to you, and how far behind they are. The lender will also want to know what percent of your total accounts receivable is owed by patients who are currently behind in their payments, as well as information on the number of patients with appropriate insurance. The accounts receivable situation is of special interest to a lender when the borrower is relying on those accounts to provide the cash flow needed to service the requested loan.

You should also expect the potential lender to ask if your practice has an adequate cash reserve to cover questionable accounts, and whether the accounts receivable have already been pledged as collateral. A lender who secures a loan with collateral that has already been pledged to a prior lender will, in most cases, be limited in its ability to foreclose on that collateral if the debtor defaults. The prior lender has first right to liquidate the collateral, while subsequent lenders will receive only those proceeds remaining after the prior debt is fully satisfied.

Fixed Assets

Since fixed assets can be used to secure the loan, the bank will likely be interested in the type, condition, age, and current market value of your equipment, machinery, and so on. You should be prepared to explain how these assets have been depreciated, their useful life expectancy, and whether they have been previously mortgaged or pledged as collateral to another lender. In addition, be ready to discuss any need or plans to acquire fixed assets. On the one hand, this need could mean additional debt obligations in the near future; on the other, it could explain and justify your projected growth.

Options for Owners of New Practices

The preceding discussion applies primarily to loan requests made by established, proven practices. New business loan applicants probably will not be able to supply much of the information described here. While this will not necessarily preclude having a new practitioner's loan approved, it could make its approval more difficult. You should, however, be aware that new business loans constitute only approximately five percent of all business loans made.

This reluctance to finance unproven businesses, understandably frustrating to new owners, is consistent with the traditionally conservative nature of banks, which owe a fiduciary duty to their stockholders and depositors to disburse funds in a prudent, responsible manner. In light of the extraordinarily high failure rate of new businesses, compounded by the fact that a new business generally cannot provide adequate financial data to evaluate its potential for success, the lender is hard pressed to justify making high-risk loans. Even where the new business borrower offers more than adequate collateral to secure the loan, the request may be denied.

Banks are comfortable lending money and earning profits from the interest charged on their loans. They are not comfortable in the role of an involuntary partner in the failing business of a delinquent debtor. Even though banks secure loans with a wide range of collateral, they understandably are not anxious to have to foreclose on that security. They are not in the business of selling medical equipment or supplies, or of trying to collect a delinquent debtor's accounts receivable. Although banks try to protect themselves by lending only a fraction of the collateral's market value, they still may not obtain the full amount that they are owed in a distress sale of that collateral, since this type of sale traditionally attracts bargain hunters who will often buy only at prices well below true market value. With an understanding of these dynamics, a loan applicant can better appreciate a bank's hesitation in approving a loan.

However, banks do make some loans to new businesses. The medical professional will need to demonstrate a good reputation for paying debts and offer evidence of business management skills. Perhaps you have firsthand knowledge and expertise in the type of practice you propose to establish as a result of having been previously involved with a similar practice. Emphasize that. In addition, provide a sound business plan to support your projections. You can further improve your chances of obtaining a loan if you have invested your own money in the practice, thus indicating your confidence in its success. Furthermore, you should show, if possible, that the practice has a good debt–equity ratio, and that it is not saddled with inordinately high debt.

Even if your loan is refused at first, it is important to establish a good working relationship with a bank. Any initial business success will impress upon the bank the soundness of your plan, thereby opening the door for future financing should the need arise.

Short-Term or Long-Term Financing?

Once the bank has evaluated the creditworthiness of your practice, you should be ready to explain the appropriateness of the kind of loan requested. I briefly mentioned this topic previously, but it deserves some additional attention. It is important to be able to convince the lender that your proposed use of the borrowed money will generate the additional revenue needed to pay the loan during the repayment period. Short-term loans are appropriate for purchasing supplies or facilitating collection of outstanding accounts receivable. They are expected to be repaid as the supplies are consumed or the accounts are collected. Long-term loans are customarily used to finance acquisition of fixed assets, which, though they may produce slow earnings initially, are expected to increase earnings in the long run. Depending upon your credit reputation, short-term loans may be available with or without security. It is more likely that long-term loans will require adequate security, often necessitating a pledge of personal and professional assets.

How Much Money Will You Need?

The lender is also concerned that the amount of the loan be adequate, since an undercapitalized practice is more likely to get into financial trouble. Similarly, a lender will be reluctant to approve a loan that is excessive, since the debt service may result in an unnecessarily high cash drain on the practice. After fees and expenses the borrower should have the amount necessary to accomplish the desired goal, with a slight cushion for error and no more. Estimating the amounts needed to finance building construction, conversion, or expansion—long-term loans—is relatively easy, as is estimating the cost of fixed-asset acquisition. On the other hand, working capital needs—short-term loans—are more difficult to assess and depend on your practice. To plan your working capital requirements, it is important to know the cash flow of your practice, present and anticipated. This involves simply a projection of all the elements of cash receipts and disbursements at the time they are likely to occur. These figures should be projected monthly to aid the bank in its evaluation.

What Kind of Collateral Do Lenders Require?

Sometimes loans will be made solely on the borrower's signature. More frequently, banks will require collateral to secure the loan. Acceptable collateral can take a variety of forms. The type and amount of collateral necessary in a given situation will depend on the particular bank's lending policies and the borrower's financial state. In general, banks will accept the following types of collateral as security for a business loan.

Endorsers', Comakers', or Guarantors' Promises to Pay

You may have to get other people to sign a note in order to bolster your credit. These people—sureties—may cosign your note as endorsers, comakers, or guarantors. While the law makes some subtle distinctions as to when each of these sureties becomes liable for the borrower's debt, in essence those parties will be expected to pay back the borrowed funds if the borrower fails to do so. The bank may or may not require sureties to pledge their own assets as security for their promise to pay upon the borrower's default. This will depend, to a great extent, on each surety's own financial situation.

Assignment of Leases

Assigning a lease as a form of security may be appropriate if your lease is assignable. Most are not.

Security Interests

Equipment loans may be secured by giving the bank a lien on the equipment you are buying. The amount loaned will likely be less than the purchase price. How much less will be determined by the present and future market value of the equipment and its rate of depreciation. You will be expected to adequately insure the equipment and to properly maintain it and protect it from damage.

Real Estate Holdings

You may be able to borrow against the equity in your personal real estate holdings as well as against those of the business. Again, you will likely be required to maintain the property in good condition and carry adequate insurance on the property for the benefit of the lender, at least up to the amount of the loan.

Accounts Receivable

Many banks will lend money secured by your business's accounts receivable. In effect, the bank is relying on your patients' ability to pay you so you can pay off your note obligation to the bank.

Savings Accounts and Life Insurance Policies

Sometimes you may get a loan by assigning your savings account to the lender. The lender will keep your passbook while notifying the savings account holder of the existence of the debt in order to ensure that the account will not be diminished during the term of the loan. Loans can also be made up to the cash value of a life insurance policy, but you must be prepared to assign the policy to the lender.

Stocks and Bonds

Stocks and bonds may be accepted as collateral for a loan if they are readily marketable. However, banks will likely lend no more than 75

percent of the market value of a high-grade security. If the value of
the securities drops below the lender's required margin, the borrower
may be asked to provide additional security for the loan.

What Are the Lender's Rules and Limitations?

Once the loan has been approved in principle, it is likely that the bank
will impose certain rules and constraints on you and your business.
These serve to protect the lender against unnecessary risk and against
the possibility of your engaging in poor management practices. You,
your attorney, and your business advisor should evaluate all of the
terms and conditions of the loan in order to determine whether it is
acceptable. If the bank's requirements are too onerous, it may be
appropriate for you to decline this loan and seek alternative financing.
Never agree to restrictions to which you cannot realistically adhere.
If, on the other hand, the terms and conditions of the loan are acceptable, even though they are demanding, it may be appropriate to take
the loan. In fact, some borrowers view these limitations as an opportunity for improving their own management techniques and business
profitability.

Especially in making long-term loans, the lender will be interested
in the net earning power of the borrowing practice, the capability of
its management, the long-range prospects of the practice, and the long-
range prospects of the health care specialty in question.

As a result of the bank's scrutiny of your practice, the kinds of
limitations imposed will depend to a great extent on the practice itself.
If the practice is a good risk, only minimum limitations need be set.
A poor risk, of course, should expect greater limitations to be placed
on it.

There are three common types of limitations you are likely to encounter.

Repayment Terms

The bank will want to set a loan repayment schedule that accurately
reflects your ability to earn revenues sufficient to meet the proposed
obligation. Risky businesses can expect shorter terms, while proven
enterprises may receive longer periods within which to repay the loan.

In addition, the interest rate may also vary depending on the risk quality of the borrower.

Use of Pledged Security

Once a lender agrees to accept collateral to secure a loan, it will understandably be keenly interested in your assurance that, should the need arise, the collateral will still be available to satisfy the debt. To this end, the lender may take actual possession of the collateral if it is stocks, bonds, or other negotiable instruments. Of course, a bank is not likely to take physical possession of a practice's fixed assets, such as X-ray machines, and remove them to the bank's vault.

There are, however, other ways by which a bank can obtain possession of your fixed assets while allowing you to use them. For example, the lender could perfect—that is, legally establish—a security interest in equipment used in your practice by filing a financing statement in the appropriate state or county office. (A security interest is the legal term for a lender's rights in collateral.) Real estate mortgages are perfected by having them recorded in the appropriate government offices. In these situations, the bank may impose restrictions on the use of the collateral and require that it be properly maintained and adequately insured. The bank may further limit or prohibit you from pledging the same collateral for any other business debts or loans.

While this may sound reasonable, you should recognize that such restrictions could seriously hamper your ability to borrow additional funds if the need arises at a future time. For example, where equipment is used as collateral, you must find out exactly how much of your equipment is involved. A bank may ask for only a portion of the equipment to secure the loan. More likely, though, the bank's security interest will extend to all of the company's equipment on hand at any given time, including any subsequently acquired equipment. Here lies the potential problem: The equipment's value may well exceed the amount of the loan that it secures. Nonetheless, you may find yourself in the position of not being able to use any of the equipment as collateral for any additional loans. In cases where this situation is likely to arise, you are well advised to consider alternative sources of collateral.

Periodic Reporting

To protect itself, a lender may require you to supply it with certain financial statements on a regular basis, perhaps quarterly or even monthly. From these statements, the lender can see if in fact the business is performing up to the expectations projected in the loan application. This type of monitoring serves not only to reassure the lender that the loan will be repaid but also to identify and help solve problems before they become insurmountable, and thus threaten the practice's continued viability.

Details of the Agreement

The loan agreement itself is a tailor-made document—a contract between the lender and borrower—that spells out in detail all the terms and conditions of the loan. The actual restrictions placed on the loan likely will be found in the agreement under a section entitled "Covenants." Negative covenants are things that you may not do without the lender's prior approval, such as incurring additional debt or pledging the loan's collateral or other business assets to another lender as collateral for a second loan. On the other hand, positive covenants spell out those things that you must do, such as carry adequate insurance, provide specified financial reports, and repay the loan according to the terms of the loan agreement. Note that—with the lender's prior consent—the terms and conditions contained in the loan agreement can be amended, adjusted, or even waived. *Remember: You can negotiate the loan terms with the lender before signing.* True, the bank is in the superior position, but legitimate lenders are happy to cooperate with qualified borrowers.

The Loan Application

Having targeted your source for funds and analyzed your practice in terms you now know lenders look at, you are ready to develop the loan request. Although most lenders will require the application to include the same standard essential information, they often differ as to the proper format of the application. Some lenders may provide suggested formats; others may require a specific format. The actual content, length, and formality will depend on the lender's familiarity with your practice, the amount of money requested, and the proposed use of the borrowed funds. A simple application form and a conversation may be adequate for your local banker. The startup practice seeking substantial funds from lenders unfamiliar with it will be required to provide much more extensive documentation, including a detailed plan of the entire practice.

The business loan applicant is typically asked to submit any or all of the following information:

1. *Personal financial statements.* These will indicate the applicant's personal net worth. This is helpful in evaluating creditworthiness and revealing potential sources of collateral, as well as estimating repayment capabilities.

2. *Recent (previous two years) and current tax returns.* Include returns for the individual and for the practice.

3. *The practice's financial statements.* These, as mentioned previously, ideally should extend back for at least two or three years, and should have been prepared and authenticated by an independent CPA. Cash flow statements and profit projections may also be requested by the lender.

4. *A business history.* This should include past profit or loss patterns, current debt–equity ratio, current and projected cash flow, and present and projected earnings.

5. *A business plan.* This should explain the proposed use of the requested funds and explain how the loan will benefit the practice. The length and content of this plan will vary according to the financial health of the applicant's practice and the amount and type of loan for which applied.

Other documentation may also be requested. The individual lender will be able to indicate what is needed in light of the given circumstances.

Importance of Communication When Problems Arise

Once a loan is approved and disbursed, the borrower must address a new set of obligations and liabilities. Of course, if all goes according to plan, the loan proceeds are invested, the practice prospers, the loan is repaid on schedule, and all parties live happily ever after. However, the business world is fraught with uncertainty. If the practice falters and revenues tumble, the borrower may not be able to meet the debt obligations. In this unfortunate event, it becomes imperative that the borrower react responsibly, viewing the lender as a potential ally in solving problems rather than as an adversary. At least initially, bankers are not eager to exercise their right to foreclose on the collateral securing the loan at the first indication that the debt may not be repaid. They likely have no experience in marketing the types of collateral involved, nor do they want to run a distress sale, which, at best, would probably bring in only a fraction of the money owed. Additionally, foreclosing against the practice's assets further decreases the bank's chance of recovering any of the unpaid balance, since the borrower, having been stripped of the means to carry on the practice, is likely to be insolvent and facing bankruptcy. Even if the lender can liquidate the collateral at its current fair market value, that value may be well below the value agreed upon when the loan was made. For these and other reasons, banks foreclose on collateral only as a last resort.

Bear in mind that, in general, lenders prefer to work with a potentially defaulting debtor to help ease the debt burden so that the borrower can overcome the problems, stay in business, and reestablish the practice's profitability. To this end, lenders, through experience, have learned to identify a variety of red flags as indications that the debtor is experiencing financial difficulty. For example, the alert is sounded when loan payments start to be made later and later each month, or when the practice's account increasingly shows checks being dishonored for insufficient funds.

When the lender sees these signals, the account may be assigned to a separate department set up within the bank to assist borrowers in overcoming problems. The bank may be willing to offer a variety of accommodations to help the borrower: repayment terms can be extended, the amount of payment due each month can be temporarily reduced, or the bank may accept repayment of interest only, until the practice has overcome its temporary difficulties. The bank may be in a position to offer advice for ways to help solve the practice's problems, particularly where poor management is the source of the difficulties.

How far and to what extent the bank will be willing to accommodate a delinquent debtor very often depends on the attitude and degree of cooperation of the debtor. Hard-pressed debtors often fail to understand the importance of establishing a cooperative, rather than adversarial, relationship with the lender. At the first sign of trouble, the borrower should take the initiative to notify the bank and explain what is being done to remedy the situation. Expecting a bank to be sympathetic to one's plight and make concessions seems unreasonable in cases where the borrower waits until the debt is long past due before approaching the lender to explain the problems. Additionally, a bank is not likely to be too sympathetic toward a borrower who fails to return phone calls and virtually disappears, always unavailable to discuss the problem with the bank.

The lender is likely to be most cooperative with a hard-pressed debtor who early on alerts the bank to the problems, explains what efforts are being made to remedy them, and keeps in close contact with the bank, informing it of current developments and of the progress made toward solution of the problems.

A favorably impressed lender can be an invaluable asset to your business, not only in granting loans but in helping you out in difficult times. Do not underestimate the need for establishing a solid professional relationship with your lender. The ultimate success and growth of your practice may well depend on it.

7

Collections

There are several ways to deal with collection problems, ranging from preventive action to initiating a lawsuit.

The general rule is that payment is due at the time services are rendered. While this rule may be subject to some technical complications that are beyond the scope of this discussion, it basically means that the medical practitioner has the legal right to demand payment in full at that moment. This assumes that no arrangement has been made between the health care provider and the patient that would allow the patient to delay payment.

If you are fortunate enough to deal with people who always pay their bills on time, the remaining portion of this chapter may be of no interest at all. However, if you have experienced delays in payment, or have had some totally uncollectible bills, you should consider the suggestions that follow.

Ways of Encouraging Payment

Cash Discounts

A simple way to encourage early payment is by offering cash discounts. The offer of a five percent cash discount for an early or even an on-time payment may be all the encouragement some patients need.

Charging Interest on Overdue Payments: Pros and Cons

The other option, which can be combined with the incentive of cash discounts, is to charge interest on payments received after the statement due date. This method involves two possible traps. First, many states still have usury laws that limit the percent of interest that can be charged. A lender who exceeds the legal interest ceiling may find that the entire debt is forfeited, all interest is forfeited, or a usury penalty is imposed.

The second possible problem is the necessity to comply with the federal Truth-in-Lending Act and the various equivalent state laws. The Truth-in-Lending Act is basically a disclosure law that requires certain terms to be included on any contract or billing that charges interest. The required disclosures have been simplified recently, and the task of compliance is further eased by the availability of preprinted forms containing the required disclosures. While many of the required terms may seem inapplicable to a simple transaction, you are well advised, if you want to charge interest, to use a form that contains all the disclosures. These forms are available from legal publishers and attorneys.

When the Payment Never Comes If neither the carrot nor the stick is effective in obtaining payment, you have several other ways to go. The first possibility is to do nothing. If the amount is small enough, you may simply decide not to pursue collection. Needless to say, if this alternative is selected, you should refrain from providing future care to that patient.

Lawsuit A second option is the instigation of a full-scale lawsuit to force payment. In many states, a formal demand for payment must be made prior to commencing a lawsuit. Moreover, this option is only practical if the outstanding debt is relatively large, since an attorney must be hired and will likely be quite expensive, particularly if the case proceeds all the way to trial.

The court fees charged for filing a case can be rather high, ranging from $40 in some states and courts to over $150 in others. The defendant(s) (the debtor) must be personally served with court papers, which costs an additional $15 to $20 or more per defendant, depending on the difficulty of the service. Lastly, if the case is won and the buyer still refuses to pay, further proceedings must be initiated at additional cost, to execute, or force payment, on the judgment received. All in all, on a moderate debt, the expense involved in a civil trial may amount to more than the debt itself.

Small Claims Court   A simpler and less expensive solution on small debts is to bring an action in small claims court. While the rules vary from state to state, all of the systems are geared toward making the process as swift, accessible, and inexpensive as possible. Moreover, most courts have staff members who help guide people through pleading in small claims court.

The major cost savings in a small claims court proceeding results from the fact that attorneys are not customarily permitted in such courts. Unless they represent themselves or a corporation, attorneys generally may not assist with completion of the necessary forms, or appear in court. Even in states where attorneys are not specifically barred by statute, the court rules are set up in such a clear, comprehensible way that an attorney is usually not needed.

A small claims action has other advantages over a conventional lawsuit; however, not all actions can be brought in small claims court. As the name implies, only claims for small amounts can be brought. The definition of *small* ranges from maximums of $500 in Arizona to $2500 in Illinois. Moreover, only actions seeking monetary damages are appropriate in small claims court; other forms of relief, such as injunction, cannot be granted.

The small claims process is comparatively swift and inexpensive. Filing fees are generally under $35. In some states, such as Arizona, if the claim is extremely small (under $50), there is no filing fee at all. In addition, in most courts, the creditor is not responsible for informing the debtor that a suit has been brought. The clerk of the court customarily mails the notice to the defendant by certified or registered mail. A small fee is generally charged to cover mailing costs.

In many states, the hearing on a small claims action may be held on a weekend or in the evening. The hearing itself is kept simple. The technical rules of evidence and of legal procedure are not followed. The judge simply hears both sides of the case and allows any evidence or the testimony of any witnesses either party has to offer. Jury trials are never permitted in small claims courts, although the defendant may be able to have the case moved to a conventional court if desiring a trial by jury.

An action in small claims court has disadvantages, too. First, the judgment is often absolutely binding, meaning neither party may appeal. Where appeal is allowed, as in the state of New York, the party wishing to challenge the judgment must show that a grave injustice has been done. This is not easy.

The other major disadvantage to a small claims action is that the judgment may be uncollectible. In many states, the usual methods of enforcing a judgment—garnishment of wages or liens against property—are unavailable to the holder of a judgment from small claims court. In other states, such as New York, enforcement action can be taken only if the debt involved is the result of a business transaction and the debtor has three other small claims court judgments outstanding.

For the most part, care in selecting those with whom you do business will minimize the need to use legal means to collect payment for services. However, if all other methods fail, small claims court is by far the least expensive and easiest way to obtain legal redress for a small outstanding debt. The drawbacks should be considered, however, before you decide to use it as a remedy.

Collection Agencies Collection agencies have become quite common and many medical practitioners have established relationships. The charge and terms vary from agency to agency, ranging from merely taking a percentage of the recovery, with others charging a higher percentage if litigation is necessary, to some requiring an upfront payment that entitles the creditor to identify a certain number of debtors for minimum collection activity without incurring additional charges. Collection agencies are customarily listed in the telephone book yellow pages, although care should be taken to evaluate the methods, skill, and reputation of the various agencies in making your selection. Both the creditor and the collection agency are subject to tight federal regulation and, in many states, state regulation regarding debt collection practices. Agencies that commit unlawful debt collection practices can subject you to liability for their wrongful acts.

Point-of-Sale Payments

Health care practitioners customarily expect to be paid at the time services are rendered. Such payment is made by the patient using currency, check, or credit card. It is, therefore, necessary for you to determine whether the currency is authentic, whether the credit card will be honored, and whether the check is going to be honored by the bank. Obviously, the cash sale is the safest way, though you should be aware that counterfeiting is not a thing of the past. Many patients are covered by insurance, and payment for services rendered to them may come directly from the insurance carrier. Unfortunately, some insurers pay the patient rather than the health care provider. In addition, the insurer may cover only a portion of the charge based on a schedule, or may deny any payment. Therefore, it is essential for you to require the patient to assume responsibility for any portion of the services not covered by the insurer. If your services are covered by the insurer, you may not collect from the patient except for co-payments, deductibles, or any unscheduled services.

Currency

Identifying counterfeit currency is usually very technical and difficult. Occasionally, however, it is simple if the counterfeiter has made a glaring error, such as using George Washington on a five-dollar bill. The federal government is quite diligent in alerting businesspeople to the presence of counterfeit currency in a particular area when it is aware of the problem. The best way to avoid being stuck with a counterfeit bill is to keep your eyes open. It is a good idea not to accept any bill larger than $50.

Credit Cards

With regard to credit card fraud, the first thing to do is to compare the signature on the back of the card with the signature on the credit card slip. Even more important is to follow the credit card company's procedures carefully. If the company requires you to get authorization for all credit card sales over $50, then be sure to get that authorization. It may seem time-consuming and troublesome, but the rules are based on bitter experience. If you have made a credit card sale without following the instructions, and the credit card turns out to have been stolen or the patient has exceeded his or her credit limit, you are likely to be stuck with the loss.

Personal Checks

The most frequent problems occur over personal checks. A host of things can prevent a check from being honored or cashed by a bank.

Accept checks only if they are made out to you and only if they are written for the exact amount of the services. In other words, do not take checks made out to someone else and endorsed to you, never *cash* a check, and do not take checks for more than the amount due—that is, when you then have to give change in cash.

One of the most common difficulties is the problem of insufficient funds to cover the check. If the amount of your bill is substantial, you might wish to request a certified or bank check. However, the inconvenience of requiring the patient to have a check certified may interfere with your relationship and is thus not practical in most situations.

If the person writing the check is known to you, it is less likely the person will give you a bad check. Even if the patient is a stranger, the risk of receiving a bad check and not being able to locate the patient afterward can be reduced if the patient's address and phone number are printed on the check.

Despite all these precautions, some bad checks do slip through. It is a crime in most states to pay for something with a check that the signer knows will be dishonored. A lawsuit can be brought against a patient to recover the amount of the check. If you win such a suit, most states will allow the recovery of reasonable costs of litigation, including the attorney's fees.

A check returned for insufficient funds can be redeposited in the hope that the check will be covered the second time through. Some bad checks are simply the result of a miscalculation of account balance, or of the patient having received and deposited a bad check. It is always a good idea to make a phone call before filing a lawsuit!

Bankruptcy

Straight Bankruptcy

There are two general categories of bankruptcy. The first, referred to as straight bankruptcy in Chapter 7 of the Bankruptcy Code, contemplates the prompt conversion of all of the bankrupt's nonexempt property to cash, and the payment of creditors to the extent possible. The Bankruptcy Code establishes a pecking order of creditors, giving some creditors priority for payment. Such creditors would be the U.S. government for taxes, and secured parties for the amount of their security interests. Each category of creditor must be paid in full before a lower-priority creditor may be paid at all. If there is not sufficient money to satisfy all creditors in a particular class, the members of that group will receive a pro rata portion of their claim.

There are some things among the bankrupt's assets that may be retained, such as a modest house, books or tools used in trade, a holy book, clothing, and the like, even after bankruptcy. The list of exempt property varies from state to state.

After the bankrupt's nonexempt assets are completely distributed, the court appointed trustee will apply to the bankruptcy judge for a discharge order. If the bankrupt has fulfilled all requirements of the Bankruptcy Code and the judge is satisfied with the proceeding, the bankrupt's debts will be wiped out—or discharged—and the proceeding will end. Certain claims, however, cannot be discharged in bankruptcy; for example, any creditor who was not notified of the bankruptcy and given a chance to participate in the proceeding will have a claim that remains viable even after the bankruptcy proceeding has ended.

Reorganization

The second type of bankruptcy proceeding is the so-called Chapter 11, or reorganization, which follows a somewhat different process. Rather than terminating the business, a Chapter 11 is designed to facilitate an orderly payment to creditors so that the business may survive.

When the Chapter 11 petition is filed and the creditors meet, a reorganization plan is proposed. All legal proceedings for debt collection other than the bankruptcy proceeding are frozen, and the bankrupt is given an opportunity to satisfy the creditors in a timely fashion. Once a plan acceptable to all creditors is prepared, it is presented to the bankruptcy judge. If it is determined that the Chapter 11 reorganization plan is "fair and equitable," the judge will approve it and it will be implemented.

Creditors customarily receive more under Chapter 11 than they do under straight bankruptcy, although reorganization is feasible only for a healthy business suffering a temporary economic reversal. Creditors who have a secured position, such as those who have filed UCC documents to establish their security interest (discussed in Chapter 6), participate in drafting the Chapter 11 plan. Generally, these creditors would be those who sold on consignment, or those who retain a security interest for the purchase price of some merchandise or equipment. A plan will be deemed fair and equitable to the secured creditors, and they may be forced to agree to it, if it provides that they will do the following:

- Retain their liens and receive future cash payments equal to the value of the security; or
- Retain a lien on the proceeds from the sale of their collateral; or
- Receive the equivalent of their interests, such as cash up front or substituted collateral.

In a Chapter 11 proceeding, a secured creditor, in order to have the plan accepted by all the creditors, may be forced to accept a less favorable position than the UCC would allow. Even though that may happen on occasion, someone with a security interest is still far better off than one who is unsecured.

Common sense, diligence, and attention to detail are always important attributes for any businessperson. When the economy is weak and money is tight, these attributes are essential. There will probably always be some uncollectible bills. But with proper care and some preventive attention, you can keep these to a minimum.

8

Renting Your Office

At some point in the life of your business, you will probably find it necessary to evaluate the terms and conditions of a commercial lease. These are much more subject to negotiation and pitfalls than residential leases, which are more tightly regulated in most states. You should consult an attorney with experience in negotiating commercial leases before signing one. This discussion is intended to alert you to some of the topics that should arise in your discussion with your lawyer.

To begin with, the exact space to be rented should be spelled out in the lease, in detail. If your space is in a professional building or office complex and you share responsibility for common areas with other tenants, these responsibilities should be explained. Will you be responsible for cleaning and maintaining them, or will the landlord? When will the common areas be open or closed? What other facilities are available to you, such as restrooms, storage, and the like?

Another important item is the cost of the space. Will you be paying a flat monthly rental or one that will change based on your earnings at the location? In order to evaluate the cost of the space, you should compare it with other similar spaces in the same locale. Do not be afraid to negotiate for more favorable terms. Care should be taken not to sign a lease that will restrict you from opening another facility close to the one being rented.

It is also important for you to consider the period of the lease. If, for example, you intend to rent only for a year or two, then you are concerned with a short term; however, it is probably still a good idea to get an option to extend. Moving can cause a lot of problems with mail and telephone numbers. Besides, if you move every year or two, some patients may feel that you are unstable, and patients who consult you only sporadically may not know where to find you after the lease period ends. Worse still, they may find a competitor in your old space.

Long-term leases are recordable in some states. Recording, where permitted, is generally accomplished by having the lease filed in the same office as a deed to property would be filed. Check with a local real estate title company or real estate attorney for the particulars in your state. If you are in a position to record your lease, it is probably a good idea to do so since you will then be entitled to receive legal and other notices that are related to the property.

It is essential for you to determine whether there are any restrictions on the particular activity you wish to perform on the leased premises. For example, there may be some restrictions on the use of X-ray equipment. Some landlords impose weight restrictions on any equipment installed in the office. It is a good idea to insist on a provision that puts the burden of obtaining any permit or variances on the landlord or, if you are responsible for them, the inability to obtain them should be grounds for terminating the lease without penalty.

Be sure the lease provides that you are permitted to use any sign or advertising on the premises, or spells out any restrictions. It is not uncommon, for example, for historic landmark laws to regulate signs on old buildings. Can you put a sign in your window or in front of your building? Some zoning laws prohibit this.

You should also be aware that extensive remodeling may be necessary for certain spaces to become suitable for your use. Be aware that the Americans with Disabilities Act requires businesses that are open to the public to be accessible to the disabled. Accessibility includes, for example, wheelchair accessibility and might require elevator buttons to be ''brailled.'' This law is quite technical and you should consult with your attorney about it before renting or purchasing an office. If this is the case, it is important for you to determine who will be responsible for the costs of remodeling. In addition, it is essential to find out whether it will be necessary for you to restore the premises to their original, pre-remodeled condition when the lease ends. This can be expensive and, in some instances, impossible. The lease should also contain a provision for parking. Will you be provided with adequate spaces for yourself, your employees, and your patients?

Who Pays for What?

If you need special hookups, such as extra water or electrical lines, you should determine whether the landlord will provide them or whether you have to bear the cost. Of course, if the leased premises already have the necessary facilities, you should question the landlord regarding the cost of these utilities. Are they included in the rent or are they to be paid separately? Are they on a separate meter or will the landlord merely pro-rate your portion of the utilities?

In some locations, garbage pickup is not a problem, since it is one of the services provided by the municipality. On the other hand, it is common for renters to be responsible for their own trash disposal. In commercial spaces, this can be quite expensive and should be addressed in the lease. Medical waste presents a special problem that should be addressed in the lease. You may have to make special arrangements for disposal.

Customarily, the landlord will be responsible for the exterior of the building. It will be the landlord's obligation to make sure that it does not leak during rainstorms and that it is properly ventilated. Notwithstanding this fact, it is important for you to make sure the lease deals with the question of responsibility if, for example, the building is damaged and some of your records or equipment is damaged or destroyed. Will you have to take out insurance for the building as well as its contents, or will the landlord assume responsibility for the building insurance?

Similarly, you should find out whether it will be your obligation to obtain liability insurance for injuries that are caused in areas of the building not under your control, such as common hallways and stairwells. You should, of course, have your own liability policy for accidental injuries or accidents that occur on your leased premises.

Security, Hours, and Zoning

A good lease will also contain a provision dealing with security. If you are renting indoor space in a medical complex, it is likely that the landlord will be responsible for external security, although this is not universally the case. If you are renting an entire building, it is customarily your responsibility to provide whatever security you deem important. Does the lease permit you to install locks or alarm systems? If this is something you are interested in, you should address the question.

Your lease should also address the issue of building hours. If you have evening or weekend clinics, your lease should specify that your patients will have ready access to your office.

Does the lease have any restrictions on deliveries, their time, or location? If you are regularly accepting deliveries, your lease should contain a provision that will give you the flexibility you require.

If the place you wish to rent will be used as both your personal dwelling and for business, other problems may arise. It is quite common for zoning laws to prohibit certain forms of commercial activities when the area is zoned residential. There is often an exception for medical professionals, but you should consult with your attorney before attempting to practice out of your home.

Finally, it is essential for you to be sure that every item agreed on between you and the landlord is stated in writing. This is particularly important when dealing with leases, since many state laws provide that a long-term lease is an interest in land and can be enforced only if in writing.

The relationship between landlords and tenants is an ancient one that is undergoing a good deal of change. Care should be taken when examining a potential business location to determine exactly what you can do on the premises and whether the landlord or municipal rules will allow you to use the location for its intended purpose.

9

Insurance

Insurance as we know it originated in a London coffeehouse called Lloyd's, sometime in the late seventeenth century. Lloyd's was a popular gathering place for seamen and merchants engaged in foreign trade. As Shakespeare pointed out in *The Merchant of Venice*, great profit can come from a successful sea voyage, but financial disaster can follow just as surely from a loss of ships at sea. From past experience, these merchants knew that, despite their greatest precautions, such disaster could strike any one of them.

Through their dealings with the Italians, the merchants had become familiar with the notion of insurance, but there was no organized insurance company in England at that time. When these merchants were together at Lloyd's, it became a custom to arrange for mutual insurance contracts. The method employed was for a ship's owner, before the ship embarked, to pass around a slip of paper that described the ship, its captain and crew, its destination, and the nature of its cargo. Those merchants who wished to be insurers of that particular ship would initial this slip and indicate the percentage of loss for which they would assume responsibility. This slip was circulated until the entire value of the ship and cargo was covered. This method of creating insurance contracts was known as "underwriting."

Today, the term underwriting is used to describe the formation of any insurance contract, regardless of the means employed in consummating it. Lloyd's of London still uses a method similar to that which originated in the coffeehouse, but most other insurance companies secure against loss out of their own financial holdings.

The risks covered by insurance have changed as well. The original Lloyd's dealt in maritime insurance only. Today, almost anything can be insured—from a surgeon's hands to a Concorde jet.

The Basics of Insurance Law

Before analyzing the mechanics of choosing whether to insure against the various risks pertinent to your business, I will briefly outline the law of insurance. All insurance is based on a contract between the insurer and the insured, whereby the insurer assumes a specified risk for a fee called a premium. The insurance contract must contain at least the following: (1) a definition of whatever is being insured (the subject matter), (2) the nature of the risks insured against, (3) the maximum possible recovery, (4) the duration of the insurance, and (5) the due date and amount of the premiums. When the amount of recovery has been predetermined in the insurance contract, it is called a valued policy. An unvalued or open insurance policy covers the full value of property up to a specified policy limit. I will be discussing the advantages and disadvantages of each in this chapter.

The insurance contract does more than merely shift the risk from the insured to the insurance company. The insurance industry is regulated by state law. Insurance companies spread the risk of a loss among those subject to the same risk. The risk-spreading is accomplished by defining the method used for determining the amount of the premium to be paid by the insured. First, the insurance company obtains data on the actual loss sustained by a class within a given period of time. State law regulates just how the company may define the class. An insurance company may not, for example, segregate caucasian homeowners and other homeowners into different classes, but it may separate drivers with many accidents from drivers with few.

Next, the company divides the risk equally among the members of the class. Then the company adds a fee for administrative costs and profits. This amount is regulated by each state's insurance regulator. Finally, the premium is set for each individual in proportion to the likelihood of a loss occurring to him or her.

Besides the method of determining premiums, state insurance laws usually specify the training necessary for agents and brokers, the amount of commission payable to them, and the kind of investments the insurance company may make with the premiums.

The very documents a company uses to create insurance contracts are regulated from state to state. Sometimes the state requires a standard form from which the company may not deviate, especially for fire insurance. A growing number of states are stipulating that plain English must be used in all forms. Plain English is measured in reference to the average number of syllables per word and the average number of words per sentence. Because of a federal ruling that all insurance contracts are per se fraudulent if they exceed certain maximum averages, the insurance companies are forced to write contracts that an average person can understand. Nevertheless, only insomniacs read most insurance forms.

Expectations versus Reality

One frequent result of the gobbledygook in which most insurance contracts are written is that the signed contract may differ in some respect from what the agent may have led the insured to expect. If you can prove that an agent actually misled you, the agent will be personally liable to you for the amount of promised coverage.

Most often, the agent will not lie but will accidentally neglect to inform the insured of some detail. For instance, if you want insurance for transporting expensive equipment, the agent may sell you a policy that covers transport only in public carriers—when you intended to rent a truck and transport the equipment yourself. In most states, the courts hold that it is the duty of the insured to read the policy before signing. If, in the preceding example, you neglected to read the clause that limits coverage to a public carrier, you would be out of luck. Failure to read the policy is not considered a valid excuse.

In other, more progressive states, this doctrine has been considered too harsh. These states will allow an insured to challenge specific provisions in the contract to the extent they do not conform to reasonable expectations resulting from promises that the agent made. In the preceding example, it might be considered reasonable to expect that you would be insured when transporting your own goods. If the agent did not specifically bring your attention to this limitation in the contract, odds are that you would have a good case for getting rid of it.

Of course, I would not advise waiting for an agent to point out these unexpected variations, even in the most liberal state. You should read the contract with the agent. If it is unintelligible, ask the agent to list on a separate sheet all the important aspects before you sign, and then keep that sheet with the contract.

Reforming the Contract

After the insurance contract has been signed, its terms can be reformed (revised) only to comply with the original agreement from which the written contract may somehow have deviated.

Let us consider the case of a woman who inherited a pearl necklace. An appraiser, apparently hoping for a large fee, misled her and told her the pearls were genuine and worth $60,000. Before having them shipped to her from the estate, she obtained insurance on them in the amount of $60,000, paying a premium of $2450. In the description of the subject matter, it was stated that the pearls were genuine. The pearls were ruined after they arrived at the delivery terminal but before she received them. She tried to collect the $60,000.

In the course of the investigation of the accident, it was discovered that the pearls were not genuine but cultured and were worth only $61.50. Of course, the insured could not collect $60,000 because no genuine pearls were lost or damaged. The worst of it was that she could not collect even $61.50 because the policy did not cover cultured pearls. The court emphasized that, for reformation of the contract to be granted, there must have been something either included or omitted contrary to the intention of both of the parties. In this case, neither party ever intended to include cultured pearls, so the court refused to make a contract for the parties covering cultured pearls.

You might think that the insured would get back her premium because there were never any genuine pearls to insure. She argued this but lost again. The court reasoned that had the pearls been lost in transit instead of being destroyed, the actual value of the pearls would have never come to light. Therefore, the insurance company had, indeed, assumed the risk of paying out $60,000 and was entitled to the premium.

Overinsuring and Underinsuring

If an insured accidentally overvalues goods, there may still be recovery. Had the pearls been genuine but worth only $20,000, the insured would have recovered $20,000. Note that overinsurance does not entitle one to recover more than the actual value of the goods insured. This is because one does not have an insurable interest beyond the actual value of an item. To allow a recovery greater than the value of the goods would be no different from allowing people to gamble with insurance policies.

Since you can at best break even with insurance, you might think it would be profitable to underinsure your property. You could gain by paying lower premiums and lose only in the event that the damage exceeds the policy maximum. This has been tried but without success.

Let us study a case where the insured stated the value of her unscheduled property as $9950 and obtained insurance on that amount. Unscheduled property means an undetermined collection of goods—for example, all a doctor's waiting room furniture and office equipment—that may change from time to time. In this case, a fire occurred, causing at least $9950 damage. (See the section "Scheduling Property" later in this chapter for further discussion of this subject.)

The insurance company investigated the claim and determined that the insured owned at least $36,500 in unscheduled property. The company refused to pay on the grounds that the insured obtained the insurance fraudulently. The court agreed with the insurance company, stating that the intentional failure to communicate the full value of the unscheduled property rendered the entire contract void. Therefore, the insured could not even collect the policy maximum. All she could hope to recover was the premiums she had paid.

Although at first glance this decision may seem harsh, its ultimate fairness becomes apparent. The chance of losing $9950 out of $36,500 is greater than the chance of losing $9950 out of $9950, simply because most accidents or thefts do not result in total losses. In this case, the insured should not have paid premiums for $9950 coverage because she belonged in a much higher risk category.

Various tests are used by the courts to determine whether an omission or misstatement renders such a policy void. In all cases, the omission or misstatement must be intentional or obviously reckless, and it must be material to the contract. Materiality is measured with reference to the degree of importance that the insurance company ascribes to the omitted or misstated fact. If stating the fact correctly would have significantly affected the conditions or premiums that the company would demand, the fact is material. In the preceding case, had the full value of the unscheduled property been stated, the insurer would either have demanded that the full value be insured or that a higher premium be paid for the limited coverage. Thus the misstatement was clearly material.

Unintentional Undervaluing

It should be noted that not all undervaluations will be material. Many insurance contracts do allow some undervaluation where it is unintentional. This provision is designed to protect the insured from inflation, which causes property to increase in replacement value before the policy's renewal date.

A so-called "coinsurance clause" generally provides that the insured may recover 100% of any loss up to the face value of the policy, provided the property is insured for a certain percentage of its value, usually 80%. For example, if a building worth $100,000 was insured for $80,000 and suffered a $79,000 loss from a covered casualty, the insured would recover the full amount of the loss, or $79,000. If the property was insured for only $50,000, a formula would be used to determine the amount of recovery. This formula is: divide the amount of insurance coverage ($50,000) by the total value of the property ($100,000) and multiply the resulting fraction (1/2) by the loss ($79,000) to get the recovery ($39,500).

This example points out the importance of carrying insurance on at least the required percentage of the value of your property. Considering the inflation rate, it is wise to reexamine your coverage each year.

All insurance policies are limited to certain defined subject matter and to losses caused to that subject matter by certain defined risks. It is a simple matter to decide whether to insure against them. Correctly defining the subject matter of insurance is tricky business. Mistakes here are not uncommon and can result in any one of us finding ourselves uninsured—like the woman with the pearl necklace.

Scheduling Property

The typical insurance policy will contain various exclusions and exemptions. For example, most homeowner and auto insurance policies cover personal property but exclude business property. If you keep certain items such as your medical bag at home, are the items personal or business property? The answer depends on whether you ever use the bag and its contents in your practice. If you do, this may convert them all to business property.

In order to avoid the potentially tragic loss of such property, you may schedule the pieces that are held for business use. Scheduling is a form of inventorying where the insured submits a list and description of all pieces to be insured with an appraisal of their value. The insurer assumes the risk of all scheduled items without concern as to whether they pertain to the business or not. Insurance on scheduled property is slightly more expensive than that of unscheduled property.

Many battles occur over the value of objects stolen, destroyed, or lost. In anticipation of such battles, you should maintain records of receipts to establish the market price of your property and an inventory of all property on hand. In the case of certain kinds of property (artwork or antiques, for example), the value must be determined by an expert in the field. However, this will not avoid all problems because the insurance company can always contest the scheduled value.

What and When to Insure

We now come to the most important issues: how to decide what should be insured and whether the risk of loss is high enough to justify an outlay for insurance premiums.

When you are uncertain as to whether something should be insured, there are several factors to consider in making your decision. First, you must set a value on that which is to be insured. Life and health are of the utmost value and should customarily be insured. Material goods are valued according to the cost of replacement. If you keep a large inventory of goods or if you own expensive equipment, it probably should be insured. The most elementary way to determine whether the value is sufficiently high to necessitate insurance is to rely on the pain factor: if it would hurt to lose it, insure it!

Second, you must estimate the chances that a given calamity will occur. An insurance broker can tell you what risks are prevalent in your particular type of practice. You should supplement this information with your personal knowledge. For example, you may know that your office is virtually fireproof. Although these facts should be weighed in your decision, you should not be guilty of audaciously tempting fate, for, as the great tragedians have recounted, to scoff at disaster is to invite it. And if the odds are truly slim but some risk is still present, the premium likely will be correspondingly smaller.

Finally, the cost of the insurance should be considered. Bear in mind that insurance purchased to cover your business is tax-deductible. (For a discussion of tax deductions and their economic impact, see Chapter 14.)

Common Areas of Concern

There are certain risks that are common to the health care industry and thus deserve special mention. These risks fall into roughly four categories: protection of your building and its contents (property insurance), protection against malpractice (professional liability insurance), protection of the health and welfare of you and your employees (health insurance), and disability insurance.

1. *Property Insurance*

The choice of insurance with respect to your building and its contents will depend on whether you own the building or are a tenant. If you are an owner, you will need to obtain insurance on your building to protect against loss from fire and possibly vandalism. If you are in an area that is prone to earthquakes, flooding, tornadoes or hurricanes, you can probably get an extended coverage endorsement (usually attached to your fire insurance policy) to cover loss under these particular circumstances. If you are leasing space, you need only consider insuring the contents of your premises.

Insurance on building contents is a separate contract, although it is usually combined with the policy on the building itself. You will want to consider obtaining fire and theft insurance on most, if not all, of your lab and office equipment, files, inventory, and so forth.

A common form of insurance obtained by professionals is "general liability" insurance. This insurance may be combined with personal and real property insurance and may include "premises liability coverage"—protection against "slip-and-fall" type injuries; "non-owned automobile coverage"—protection against liability for auto accidents that occur during work hours but in a privately owned car (for example, if an employee uses his or her car to deliver X-ray film to a hospital and gets in an accident while on the way back to your office); and "employee negligence coverage"—protection against negligent acts committed by your employees (this is not professional liability insurance!).

2. *Professional Liability Insurance*

It is no secret that malpractice claims have become one of the occupational hazards of the health care industry. The medical profession has probably seen the greatest increase in malpractice claims. A 1987 report released by the Department of Health and Human Services showed that claims made against physicians rose from three per 100 prior to 1981 to ten claims per 100 in 1985. In 1991, the number of claims had risen to 13.9 per 100. Although medical professionals are the most susceptible to malpractice claims, all health care professionals are exposed to potential liability. One successful claim can wipe you out if you are not properly insured. Consequently, professional liability insurance should be considered a necessity.

Professional liability insurance is quite complex. Due to the extreme importance of maintaining sufficient coverage, it is highly advised that you consult with a local attorney who is knowledgeable in the field of malpractice and insurance defense. There are two important issues you need to be familiar with before consulting an attorney and obtaining coverage.

(a) *Coverage.* Malpractice, as discussed in Chapter 10, results when an injury is sustained due to a practitioner's substandard care. Professional liability insurance covers claims arising only from such substandard care. It will not cover intentionally injurious or criminal acts. It does not cover acts of sexual misconduct. It usually does not cover claims arising from injuries sustained from improperly maintained premises (office, waiting room, and parking lot, for example)—although a general liability policy (discussed above) should.

A professional liability policy may cover negligent acts committed by your employees within the scope of their employment. Since you may be liable for such acts, it is important that you check your policy to see whether you are covered, or whether your employees should be identified as "additional insureds" under the policy.

Policies vary with respect to the costs that are covered. Some policies cover only the actual damages awarded to the successful claimant (patient). Other policies also cover the cost of defending against the malpractice claim. The difference can be critical. For example, assume that a practitioner has $1,000,000 worth of coverage which covers *only* damages actually awarded. The patient successfully brings a malpractice suit and recovers $700,000 in damages. The attorney's fees for defending the practitioner total $120,000. Even though the practitioner is covered well in excess of the damages award and attorney's fees, the practitioner is *personally* liable for the $120,000 owed to the attorney. Defending malpractice suits is generally very expensive, so check to make sure that your policy covers the costs of litigation. Policies that do not include attorney's fees are extremely rare.

Practitioners frequently ask "How much coverage do I need?" There is no formula that dictates how much insurance is enough, although a common answer is "Enough to allow you to sleep at night!" Generally, medical practitioners carry the most protection. "Noninternists" (family practitioners, for example) generally carry anywhere from $1,000,000–$2,000,000 coverage. Specialists, surgeons, and other high-risk practitioners (such as anesthesiologists) typically carry more. Licensed medical professionals other than physicians, such as dentists and nurse-practitioners, have considerably less coverage because of the decreased amount of risk and a lesser likelihood of irreparable harm associated with these professions. It is important to remember that the best insurance is to maintain a proper standard of care—you could easily go broke trying to keep "enough" insurance coverage. A hospital, clinic, or practice plan may specify certain coverage amounts that must be carried.

There are certain coverage limits to be aware of. Coverage may be limited to the policy's effective period, or it may be limited on a per-person basis. To illustrate, assume the policy is for $1,000,000 worth of coverage for one year. If it is limited on a period basis, the policy will cover any claim(s) made during that year, up to an aggregate of $1,000,000. If it is limited on a per-person basis, on the other hand, the policy will cover $1,000,000 worth of claims *per person* made during that year. Such a policy will have a cap—say, up to $5,000,000—so that a thoroughly incompetent practitioner does not bankrupt the insurer.

(b) *Types of Policies.* There are two types of professional liability policies—"occurrence" and "claims-made." Occurrence policies have become less common in recent years. Due to the nature of their coverage, carriers have been less inclined to write such policies.

An occurrence policy covers claims that *occur* during the period of coverage. For example, say that a practitioner is covered from January 1, 1992 through December 31, 1992 (one year, for simplicity's sake) and he or she improperly delivers a child on June 1, 1992. Regardless of when a claim is finally made, the practitioner is covered. Complications may not develop for many years, yet the policy will retroactively cover the claim since the event *occurred* during the period of coverage. This possibility of "delayed liability" is precisely why many carriers refuse to write such policies. Those who do generally charge a proportionately higher premium than for a comparable amount of claims-made coverage.

Claims-made policies are limited to claims that are actually made during the period of coverage. Assume the facts as above. Complications, as a result of the improper delivery, do not develop until January 1, 1995, at which time a malpractice claim is filed. Since the practitioner was covered by a claims-made policy only during 1992, the claim is *not* covered, even though the act of malpractice occurred during the period of coverage. Since it is common for complications to develop years after an act of malpractice has occurred, it is important that there not be any gaps in your claims-made coverage.

Gaps in insurance coverage may occur when you take an extended sabbatical or retire from the profession altogether. If you have been covered during your entire practice by an occurrence policy, there is no cause for concern regarding potential gaps in your policy. There are two scenarios where gaps in coverage commonly occur.

First, if you are converting a claims-made policy into an occurrence policy at the end of the earlier policy's life, you will need to obtain "nose coverage" attached to the occurrence policy, as well as the occurrence policy itself, to cover a gap that now exists. Nose coverage protects against acts of malpractice that have *occurred* prior to the beginning of the occurrence policy, but for which no claim is made until after the claims-made policy has ended. As an alternative you could purchase "tail" coverage for the claims-made policy, which, in essence, extends the coverage for that policy.

Second, a gap in coverage will occur where you have been covered by a claims-made policy up to a particular point in time, at which time you no longer need coverage (for example, you are retiring, changing insurers, or stepping down your practice to a lower-risk specialty), so the policy is terminated. If an act of malpractice occurred during your practice, but a claim is made after you have retired, you will not be covered unless you obtain "tail coverage." Tail coverage protects against claims that arise after an earlier policy has lapsed or been terminated. Both nose and tail coverage can be expensive—from one-and-one-half to two times your annual premium—but are necessary to prevent gaps in coverage from occurring. Many policies provide some "tail" coverage free of charge if you have been insured for an extended period of time. It is a good idea to review your professional liability coverage each year. Waiting to find out that your coverage is inadequate until a claim is made would be disastrous.

3. *Health Insurance*

Employers often provide health benefits (medical, dental and/or vision coverage) to their employees as an employment benefit. If you choose to provide this benefit, it is unwise for you to render health care to your employees in lieu of purchasing insurance. In the unlikely event of unsatisfactory treatment, the relationship between you and your employee would be jeopardized. Therefore, it is more prudent to obtain insurance coverage for your employees' health, dental, and vision needs and insist that they seek treatment from another practitioner. With the ever-increasing prevalence of managed care organizations, many employers have turned to policies written by one of the popular health maintenance organizations (HMOs) or preferred provider organizations (PPOs) for their employee health care needs.

4. *Disability Insurance*

The importance of including disability insurance as a part of your benefit program cannot be overemphasized. Disability may be characterized as a "living death." This characterization is appropriate when considering that the professional's financial needs remain constant or may even increase, while earnings potential is curtailed.

While it is theoretically possible for the individual to establish a savings program so that funds will be available in the event of a disabling occurrence, in reality such a "self-funded" program is impractical. The obstacles to such an approach include tax laws, with their current bias against savings and timing. The implementation of a savings program takes time, which could be interrupted by a disability or by other requirements for those funds.

Accordingly, the most practical method of accommodating this need is through the acquisition of a disability insurance policy. There are two general types. The first provides benefits through a group contract. This is similar in many respects to group term life insurance. The second category is policies issued directly to individuals. These may be funded directly by individual employees or by the employer.

There are tax considerations that might influence your selection of a particular type of program, and you are well advised to consult with your tax adviser and a financial planner with expertise in employee benefit programs before making your selection. The contracts themselves contain numerous complex terms and involve careful planning. Your professional advisers should be able to evaluate the various policies and their terms and recommend the one that best fits your situation.

Keeping Insurance Costs Down

As previously discussed, the premiums charged by insurance companies are determined by law. Nonetheless, it still pays to shop around. Insurance companies compete by offering a variety of different packages.

10

Malpractice

The term "medical malpractice" has been overused to describe many different forms of misconduct. Ethical violations, fraud, breach of fiduciary duty, battery, and invasion of privacy are the most common forms of misconduct that are frequently referred to as malpractice. But medical malpractice is really just a specialized form of negligence, called "professional negligence."

There are numerous texts and multivolume treatises that are available for an in-depth discussion of medical malpractice. My purpose here, however, is to give the practitioner a general overview to aid in making decisions that will reduce exposure to liability. In this chapter, I will discuss: (1) the factors courts consider in determining whether a practitioner has committed malpractice, (2) the defenses that are available once a claim has been made, and (3) the problem of your liability for the wrongful acts of others.

Negligence is a term used to describe a basis for liability that results from a failure to perform some duty that the law requires, under a given set of circumstances. Generally, the duty that the law imposes is a duty to use "due care," or to "exercise the prudence that a reasonable person would exercise in similar circumstances."

For example, it is considered negligent for a person who has extremely poor vision to attempt to drive without glasses, based on the theory that a "reasonable person" would not attempt to drive under the circumstances. Professional negligence is simply an extension of the negligence theory to circumstances where an individual is held to a higher standard of care as a result of special skills or knowledge that he or she holds himself or herself out as possessing.

In order for a patient to prevail on a claim of professional negligence, he or she must prove that there was some duty flowing from the health care provider to the patient, that the duty was breached, and that the patient was injured as a result.

The duty that flows from the health care professional to the patient arises as a consequence of the relationship between the two parties. By accepting responsibility for treatment, the practitioner impliedly represents (and the law imposes a duty) that he or she will use reasonable care and diligence in the exercise of the advanced skills and knowledge he or she possesses, to accomplish the purpose for which employed.

The duty owed to the patient is that the practitioner will conform to a certain accepted standard of medical care. It is this standard against which the practitioner's conduct is judged to determine whether or not the practitioner is liable for professional negligence.

The Standard of Care

All persons are held to certain minimum standards in the activities they undertake. However, if a person acquires special competence, he or she is held to a standard commensurate with his or her superior knowledge and skills. Consequently, since health care professionals possess knowledge, skills, and training superior to that of the ordinary person, the law imposes a higher standard of care upon them.

The standard of care to which health care professionals are held is measured by "the degree of knowledge, skill, and care ordinarily possessed and employed by members of the profession in good standing." Obviously, the kind of conduct required will vary between the different health care professions, depending on the standard of care customarily exercised by members of that branch of the profession. In addition, if the practitioner holds himself or herself out as a specialist in a particular field, he or she will be required to act as a reasonably competent specialist in the same or similar circumstances.

Regardless of the particular field of health care, the practitioner is not required to be endowed with extraordinary knowledge and skill. But he or she is required to keep abreast of the times and to practice in accordance with recognized methods of treatment.

Whether or not a practitioner has deviated from the accepted standard of care is largely dependent upon the particular facts of each case. The law recognizes that many times, under a given set of facts, there may be more than one acceptable method of treatment that meets the standard of care. Consequently, the practitioner is not judged in hindsight; that is, liability cannot be based on the fact that it later appears that another approach would have been more successful. The practitioner is entitled to have the propriety of his or her conduct judged according to the practices of the particular "school of medicine" to which the practitioner belongs. Courts have held that the "school" must be recognized and that a "respectable minority" of practitioners must follow the principles, in order for the school to be legitimate. However, the practitioner must still properly administer the particular school's techniques; the practitioner cannot conceal his or her incompetence behind a veil of professional opinion.

In a dwindling minority of states, courts also give consideration to the particular "type of community" in which the practitioner practices when determining whether the standard of care has been met. In other words, if the practitioner practices in a remote rural area, where equipment and facilities are inferior to those of more urban areas, the practitioner's conduct will be judged according to the standard of practitioners in that (or a similar) rural community, not against other practitioners in general. This rule has fallen into disfavor over the years as technological advances in communication and transportation have made access possible to even the most remote areas. In addition, many practitioners are now board-certified in accordance with national standards.

Breach of Duty

The practitioner is required to carefully and completely utilize his or her knowledge and skill in an attempt to diagnose and treat the patient's ailment. An honest error in judgment, made in the course of following a procedure or course of treatment, that is recognized as acceptable within the particular school of medicine does not create liability.

Liability arises only when the practitioner breaches the standard of care. A breach of the standard occurs where the practitioner deviates from the recognized standards of care. Examples of conduct that would breach the requisite standard of care include performance of an unauthorized operation not justified by a medical emergency, commission of a technical error during a surgical procedure, a failure to obtain a proper medical history, failure to refer a specialist where one is necessary, failure to carefully conduct a thorough physical examination, and failure to timely diagnose a condition.

Of course, if no damage results from the practitioner's deviation from the standard of care, there can be no liability. Likewise, the patient must prove that the particular breach of duty was the substantial contributing "cause" of the injury.

Whether or not a particular act or omission is the substantial contributing cause of an injury is often a very complex issue to resolve. Essentially, the decision is arrived at by use of expert testimony.

To illustrate, suppose a physician prescribes a drug without determining whether the patient will have any adverse reactions. The patient later operates an automobile and blacks out while at the wheel. The patient's car runs into a power pole, causing a blackout in a nearby city, where a person falls down the stairs in the dark and breaks his leg. The practitioner would certainly be liable for any injury to the patient, but is the practitioner also liable to the individual who broke his leg? Granted, the facts in this scenario are somewhat farfetched, but the example serves to illustrate the complexities that the causation issue raises.

Only where an aggrieved patient has proven all of the necessary factors can he or she recover monetary damages from the practitioner. In addition to civil liability to the patient, a practitioner guilty of malpractice may also face license suspension or revocation.

Informed Consent

An increasing number of malpractice cases have involved the doctrine of "informed consent." Health care professionals are required to provide their patients with sufficient information to permit the patient to make well-informed decisions regarding their treatment. Treatment without full disclosure of material risks and viable alternatives involved is another form of professional negligence.

Generally, a claim will arise where the patient consents based on insufficient information and later suffers damage as a result. The patient then brings suit, alleging that consent would not have been given had he or she been better informed of the risks involved. The procedure may have been perfectly performed, yet due to the fact that the patient was not fully informed of the material risks and viable alternatives involved, the practitioner may be liable for any adverse consequences that are normally considered an accepted risk or side effect of the procedure.

Under the doctrine of informed consent, the health care provider has a duty to explain the nature of the procedure to inform the patient of the material risks and viable alternatives involved with the proposed treatment as well as the possible alternative forms of treatment that may be available. An injured patient must prove that the practitioner failed to provide an explanation of the procedure and the material risks and viable alternatives at issue. In addition, the patient must prove that he or she would not have undergone treatment had he or she known of the risk of harm that, in fact, occurred.

The duty to inform is not absolute under all circumstances; there are some limitations. The most significant limitation is that the risk at issue must be "material" (or significant enough) to trigger the duty to inform. Most courts today test materiality in terms of whether a reasonable person *in the patient's position* would be likely to attach significance to the risk(s) in deciding whether or not to undergo the proposed treatment (the so-called "objective test"); a minority of states still test materiality from the *individual's perspective*—whether this patient would have consented to this procedure had he/she been fully informed (the "subjective test"). Whether the patient will attach significance to the risk is determined by weighing the likelihood of a particular injury occurring, along with the seriousness of that injury. If the risk of serious injury is high, the practitioner will be compelled to disclose the information.

Unfortunately, the test(s) courts use to determine whether a risk is material do not provide a real "bright line" answer to the question of whether to disclose the risk. Consequently, the safest decision is to always provide the patient with complete information regarding (1) the actual procedure of the treatment to be undertaken, (2) the fact that there may be risks and what those risks are, and (3) the fact that there may be alternative forms of treatment, including the risks posed by the alternative form of treatment. Appropriate documentation in the medical chart, or use of well-drafted forms is important to establish that the necessary information was provided to the patient in order to obtain the informed consent.

Other limitations on the informed consent doctrine include what is known as a "therapeutic privilege" to withhold information, where disclosure of the risk would be detrimental to the well-being of the patient. For example, a surgeon may not want to disclose to his suicidal patient that the operation about to be performed will most likely result in sterilization. This becomes a matter of professional judgment. However, the practitioner should tell a relative (or legal guardian) of the probable risks involved. Again, you are well advised to document, in the chart, such withholding of information.

The practitioner is not required to disclose risks where an emergency situation precludes the practitioner from making disclosure (for example, where the patient needs immediate attention and he or she is unconscious, or is a minor or incompetent and the parent or guardian is not present). Nor is the practitioner required to disclose risks that are immaterial, obvious, or already known to the patient, or are remote.

It should be noted that in many states, a practitioner will be liable for battery where treatment is *completely unauthorized* yet performed anyway. For example, a physician who removed a patient's tonsils without consent during surgery on the patient's nose was found liable for battery. This situation differs from the informed consent cases since the treatment is administered *without any form of consent* from the patient.

Defenses

Health care professionals are not required to be the guarantors of all diagnoses and cures, unless they have promised to be—a risky proposition. As was indicated earlier, some latitude is afforded for honest mistakes in judgment. In addition, there are several defenses to a claim of professional negligence.

All states have what are known as ''good samaritan'' statutes. These statutes were enacted to encourage persons to give aid to others in emergency situations, and therefore in the majority of states are applicable to nonmedical persons as well. The statutes vary from state to state, but attempt to limit, in some way, a good samaritan's liability under emergency circumstances. The good samaritan defense is generally not available away from the scene of the emergency. In addition, in most states the person giving aid must be acting in good faith. This requirement generally has been interpreted to mean that the person giving aid must not be guilty of gross negligence.

Contributory negligence is another available defense. Contributory negligence is conduct by the patient that contributes to the cause of and/or aggravates his or her own injuries. For example, assume that a patient sees a bone specialist, complaining of pain in his shoulder. The specialist negligently fails to diagnose a fracture but advises the patient to see his family physician. The patient fails to see his family physician and later suffers complications from the fracture. If the patient later sues the bone specialist for negligence, the specialist can raise contributory negligence as a defense.

In a few states, contributory negligence is a complete bar to any recovery by the patient. Consequently, in the above example, the patient would be denied any monetary recovery if a jury were to determine that he was contributorily negligent.

In other states, the defense is known as ''comparative negligence,'' which falls into two categories. The first, known as ''pure comparative fault,'' permits the plaintiff to recover, regardless of his or her fault, so long as the defendant is responsible for at least 1 percent of the fault. This standard is used in many states including Washington and in admiralty cases. Under the second standard, which has been adopted in Oregon and many other states, the plaintiff may not recover at all if he or she is equally or more at fault than the defendant. Under the ''pure comparative fault'' standard, instead of absolutely denying the patient recovery, the award is generally reduced by an amount commensurate with the percentage of negligence attributable to the patient. On facts similar to the previous example, an actual jury found that the patient was 60 percent responsible for his injuries and therefore reduced the award by that much.

Finally, all states have statutes of limitation, which put a time limit on when a lawsuit for malpractice may be brought. These statutes vary among the states. In addition, the rules vary as to when the statute "tolls," or begins to run. Consequently, it is advisable to consult with your attorney on this and other matters that relate to professional liability.

Vicarious Liability

Vicarious liability, or liability for the mistakes of others, is an issue that occasionally arises in the area of professional malpractice. In the private practice setting, where two or more practitioners treat the same patient, neither is liable for the negligence of the other unless there is a "concert of action" between the practitioners.

For example, where a dentist determines that a patient needs his wisdom teeth removed and refers the patient to an oral surgeon for the procedure, the dentist will not be liable for any negligent acts committed by the oral surgeon. Had the dentist and the surgeon acted jointly, each would be liable regardless of the fact that one or the other had a more active role in the procedure.

Normally, a hospital staff physician is not liable for the negligence of hospital employees; however, under certain circumstances the physician will be liable. This occurs when the hospital employee is acting under the direct supervision of the physician, such as a scrub nurse in the operating room. In this case, both the employer hospital and the physician can be held liable.

Unfortunately, the law provides little guidance in determining when action is or is not "joint action." Incorporating the practice can reduce the problem of vicarious liability in the majority of states. This issue is further developed in the "Professional Corporation" section of Chapter 1.

The majority of health care professionals will adhere to the high standards of their respected professions and do everything in their power to avoid acts that might be considered malpractice. Unfortunately, unexpected problems occasionally arise. One of the best ways to avoid liability is to be aware of the current state of the law on the subject and to maintain complete and legible patient records. As with most areas of law, when you perceive the possibility of a problem, it is essential to immediately seek professional assistance from an attorney who specializes in the field of medical malpractice defense. Customarily, the attorney will be provided by your malpractice insurance carrier, or you might want to contact your professional association for some recommendations.

11

Licensing and Hospital Privileges

Health care professionals, like most other professionals, must acquire and maintain a license to practice their profession. The license serves as a symbol of that person's qualification to practice in a particular field of health care.

The license is not a right. Successful completion of the required education and/or training does not entitle the practitioner to a license. A professional license is a privilege. And like any other privilege, it can be suspended, revoked, or denied, for any of several reasons.

In this chapter I will provide a broad overview of the licensing process, including licensing requirements and reasons for license denial, suspension, or revocation. In addition, I will discuss the relationship between practitioners and hospitals, commonly referred to as "staff privileges."

A Privilege, Not a Right

As noted above, the license to practice medicine, dentistry, chiropractic, and other so-called "healing" professions is bestowed as a matter of privilege. It is not a contract with the state. It merely signifies that the practitioner has complied with the procedural requirements and possesses the necessary qualifications and that he or she is granted the privilege to practice in that particular state. Once the license has been obtained, the practitioner does not then gain an unrestricted right to practice. The state still has the power to restrain and/or regulate the practitioner during the course of his or her practice.

Each state has its own licensure requirements. Usually, a Board of Examiners or some other administrative agency oversees the licensing process. Generally, each discipline of the healing arts has a corresponding examining board, for example, the Board of Dentistry. Some states have boards that oversee more than one discipline. For example, Oregon's Board of Medical Examiners oversees the licensing of physicians (MDs and DOs), podiatrists, acupuncturists, respiratory health care technicians, and physician's assistants. Each state's statutes prescribe which of the healing arts require licensure. Most states require a license to practice as a physician, surgeon, dentist, nurse, chiropractor, optometrist, or the like. In addition, many statutes provide exemptions from the licensure requirements. For example, in many states the licensure statutes of state A do not apply to a practitioner who is licensed in state B but is in state A for purposes of consultation with another practitioner who *is* licensed in state A.

Licensure Requirements

Since licensure is regulated at the state level, the requirements will vary from state to state. It would be impractical to discuss each state's various requirements in this book. You are advised to check with your own state licensing board for the specific, detailed requirements of your state.

Though state licensing statutes do not generally say that only "natural persons" may acquire a license, most states have held this by implication; therefore, corporations generally are not allowed to acquire a license to practice a healing art; only humans may.

Most, if not all, statutes require that the applicant possess the intellectual fitness and qualification to practice a particular branch of health care. Generally, this is evidenced by completion of a professional education. In many states, a diploma from a qualifying institution serves as evidence of the fitness and qualification of the applicant to practice. Some states have more specific requirements, which dictate that certain courses must be satisfactorily completed and/or a certain number of hours of education are necessary to establish fitness and qualification.

Most states require proof of moral fitness as well. The applicant must be of solid character—trustworthy, reliable, and so forth. Acts of "moral turpitude" (theft, for example) committed in the past may disqualify the applicant from acquiring a license.

Many states require the satisfactory completion of an examination given by the appropriate Board of Examiners. Such examinations differ with regard to content, scope, and so forth. Some are written, some are oral, and some are a combination of both. Some states also require proof that the applicant has obtained professional liability (malpractice) insurance as a prerequisite to licensure. Most, if not all, states require the payment of a fee to obtain the license. The fee is administrative and covers the cost of investigation of the applicant, examination fees, and the like. Finally, most states have reciprocity provisions, which may enable licensed practitioners from other states to practice in the licensing state without the necessity of complying with all of the "first-time applicant" procedures.

Once the Board of Examiners has all of the relevant documentation and information, it makes a decision whether to grant the applicant a license. If the license is denied, a satisfactory explanation must be given to the applicant. The applicant may or may not then have an opportunity to be heard at a hearing. State licensing boards are subject to the prohibitions of the U.S. Constitution. Consequently, licensing decisions may not be based upon impermissible or discriminatory reasons such as an applicant's race or sex.

Denial, Suspension, or Revocation of a License to Practice

The denial, suspension, or revocation of a license must be based on the premise that the applicant or practitioner is or has become unfit to practice. Since the license is only a privilege, denial or revocation for good cause is universally accepted as legal.

1. *Denial*

A license may be denied for various reasons. If the applicant fails to meet any of the qualifying requirements or criteria, the license can be denied. The licensing board may not deny a license based on discriminatory reasons. Obviously, if a denial were based partially on the fact that the applicant was a member of a minority race, the denial would be a violation of the applicant's constitutional rights.

2. *Revocation and Suspension*

In order for a licensing board to suspend or revoke a license, there must be a showing of "good cause," or sufficient grounds. Each state has the power to define by statute what forms of conduct, if engaged in, will result in license revocation or suspension (as well as criminal liability in some instances). Some states have held that revocation may be based only on the acts proscribed by statute. That is, a practitioner cannot have his or her license revoked for a reason not specifically set forth within the statute.

As the qualification requirements vary between the states, so do the grounds for revocation. Immoral or unprofessional conduct is a common ground for revocation in most, if not all, states. It is also the most difficult to establish. Most courts and licensing boards have construed these statutes to mean that a breach of professional ethics or a "minor" act of unprofessional conduct does not justify license revocation.

Conduct that has been held to be unprofessional and resulted in license revocation includes the following:

- The fraudulent representation that the patient has a disease or ailment in order to extort a fee;
- The fraudulent representation that the practitioner can cure an incurable disease solely to extract a fee;
- Immoral acts committed against women patients (such as having a sexual relation);
- False or misleading advertising (although a practitioner's use of advertising in violation of local ethical rules is generally not grounds for revocation).

A practitioner can also lose his or her license for repeated acts of incompetence (generally, an isolated incident is not grounds for revocation unless it was a gross error). When the quality of treatment administered to a particular patient is called into question, the licensing board (or in some states, the disciplinary board) may hold a hearing or "contested case proceeding." The practitioner's course of treatment with respect to that patient is scrutinized and, if it is determined that the practitioner engaged in negligent conduct, the board can impose punishment ranging from probation to license revocation (depending on the severity of the error).

Most statutes provide for revocation of a license that was initially procured through fraud or misrepresentation, for example, where a practitioner misrepresents that he has never engaged in or been arrested for acts of moral turpitude, when in fact he has.

Revocation is required in many states where the practitioner allows and/or aids an unlicensed person to practice. For example, where practitioner A employs practitioner B from out of state and B is not licensed to practice in A's state (regardless of whether licensed in his own state), A would be guilty of aiding the unlicensed practice of health care and B would be guilty of practicing without a license.

Practicing under an assumed or false name is grounds for revocation in most, if not all, states. Likewise, the false designation of title—that is, that the practitioner is licensed to practice a particular specialty, when in fact he or she is not—is also almost universally grounds for revocation.

Where a practitioner has engaged in proscribed conduct that warrants revocation of his or her license, the licensing board may have the option of suspending the license instead of revoking it. Usually, the board will recommend suspension instead of revocation where mitigating circumstances demand leniency, for example, where a practitioner makes a misrepresentation out of ignorance as opposed to being willful. The practitioner's license is reinstated at the end of the suspension period, at which time he or she may resume practice.

Hospital Privileges

Most practitioners, especially physicians and surgeons, rely on the use of hospital facilities. Generally, hospitals have newer and better equipment, facilities for overnight stays, special treatment centers for such things as burns and other serious injuries, obstetrics, and so forth.

The staggering cost of equipping such facilities prohibits practitioners from acquiring most of this equipment for their own office or clinic use. Consequently, use of a hospital's facilities is often a necessity in order for many practitioners to provide patients the best possible treatment.

Just as a state is not obligated to grant a license to practice to anyone who requests it, neither is a hospital compelled to grant "staff privileges" to any practitioner who requests them. Nor is a hospital bound to extend privileges indefinitely once initially granted. Usually, hospitals deny or revoke staff privileges for many of the same reasons that a license to practice may be denied or revoked. Hospitals also deny or revoke privileges because the practitioner fails to follow hospital rules and regulations.

Unless a state statute provides otherwise, hospitals have the power to adopt reasonable regulations regarding the qualifications necessary for admission to practice at, and use, the hospital's facilities. Such discretion is necessary in order for hospitals to maintain acceptable standards of care and protect against the risk of exposure to malpractice suits. Such discretion, if left unchecked, can be and has been abused. Therefore, some limitations have been placed on a hospital's discretion to grant, deny, and revoke staff privileges.

Generally, this discretion has been regulated by the courts rather than by statutes. The degree of discretion granted is customarily dependent upon whether the hospital is publicly or privately owned.

1. *Public Institutions*

Publicly owned (nonprofit) hospitals have very little discretion in denying staff privileges. This limited discretion also applies to private hospitals that are partially funded by government funds. In the majority of states, licensed, competent practitioners may not be excluded from the use of public facilities. Such hospitals do have the right to deny or revoke staff privileges based on reasonable, nondiscriminatory grounds, such as a practitioner's prior history of incompetence or unprofessional conduct.

2. *Private Institutions*

Where a hospital has been constructed with and maintained *purely* by private dollars, it has a fairly broad discretion to pick and choose to whom it will extend staff privileges. Such hospitals have the right to exclude highly competent, licensed practitioners for a variety of reasons. For example, the hospital may choose to exclude a practitioner simply because of his or her field of specialty. So long as the decision to deny or revoke staff privileges is not based on unreasonable, arbitrary, or unlawful discriminatory grounds, the practitioner is left with little recourse.

In some states (including Colorado, Florida, Pennsylvania, and Texas, among others), both private and public hospitals may exclude *all* practitioners who practice a certain "system" of treatment. For example, hospital policy may dictate that no chiropractors may use hospital facilities. In other states, however, such discriminatory treatment, even though applied consistently, has been held to be illegal.

3. *Procedural Rights*

When a recommendation to revoke or deny privileges has been made, the practitioner has certain "due process" rights as provided in the medical staff bylaws, specifically, the right to receive notice of the charges against him or her that have culminated in the revocation or denial, and the right to be heard at an informal hearing.

Practitioners who have been subject to a recommendation to have staff privileges revoked by a public hospital may have greater rights following the recommendation. The practitioner must be given notice of the pending action and the reasons therefor prior to revocation of staff privileges. In addition, the practitioner must be given a hearing and an opportunity to participate.

Fewer procedural rights may be accorded to a practitioner who has had staff privileges recommended to be revoked or denied at a private hospital. In either case, the practitioner's rights when he/she is the subject of a recommendation to revoke or deny privileges will be governed by the medical staff bylaws. Recently, the Federal Health Care Quality Improvement Act of 1986 (Wyden Act, 42 U.S.C. 11111 et seq.) was passed, which provides the hospital and the physicians participating in a professional review action limited liability exposure to antitrust claims arising out of the peer review process if the hospital grants the aggrieved practitioner certain procedural safeguards. (Peer review is discussed more fully in the following section.) The Act is not mandatory, but an overwhelming majority of private hospitals have adopted the Act to acquire the benefits of limited liability against antitrust claims. If the hospital has adopted the Act, it *must* provide the affected practitioner a hearing in accordance with the Act's provisions.

Peer Review

Peer review is the process by which a hospital's medical staff members review the quality of care administered by fellow practitioners. A peer review committee is made up of staff practitioners from the hospital and others as provided in the medical staff bylaws. Generally, each medical staff member of the hospital will undergo peer review at some point. Usually, a recommendation to revoke staff privileges is the result of a medical executive committee's investigation. The hospital's Board of Directors makes the final decision.

Where one of the peer review panel members is in direct economic competition with the practitioner whose care has been called into question, anticompetition claims are common (for example, where an ophthalmologist is being reviewed by a panel that is comprised of one or more ophthalmologists in direct economic competition). As previously discussed, the Wyden Act limits the participating practitioner's liability if the proper procedures are followed.

The practitioner–hospital relationship is much more complex than this cursory discussion may lead one to believe. You should consult with a health law expert for a more in-depth analysis of the various rules, rights, and responsibilities that exist. In addition, as previously mentioned, the licensing laws vary widely from state to state. For specific details on your state's laws, check with the local chapter of your professional association. You can also find the licensing rules in your state's administrative rules or state statutes.

12

Patient Records

A good recordkeeping system is imperative if a medical practice is to be run effectively and efficiently. Accurate, up-to-date, and orderly records are necessary for providing appropriate health care to the patient, as well as for business and legal purposes (such as managing employees, preparing income tax records, verifying payments made, billing and collections). In this chapter and the next, we will discuss the unique issues that arise in a medical practice with respect to both medical records and business records, including the fundamentals of setting up a bookkeeping system.

Medical Records

The medical record is a compilation of information gathered from many sources, for the general purpose of assisting the medical practitioner in providing the appropriate health care to a patient. More specifically, the Joint Commission on Accreditation of Health Care

Organizations (JCAHO) suggests that the medical record serves several important purposes: It provides a basis for planning and continuity in a patient's care, it documents communications between the patient and the physician, and it provides evidence of the course of the patient's diagnosis, condition, and treatment.

The medical record also serves important functions that are not directly related to administering care to the patient. The medical record has been referred to as the physician's best friend, for it provides substantive evidence of the physician's course of treatment and conduct with respect to a given patient, for use in the defense of potential malpractice claims. In addition, if the quality of the physician's care is called into question by a state licensing board, a thorough medical record that details the physician's observations and analysis can be used to rebut a charge of incompetence and/or substandard care. It can also be used for medical research under certain circumstances.

There are essentially two categories of medical records, "primary" and "secondary." The primary record is the original medical record, which is generally composed of the patient chart, X rays, clinical test results, photographs, sketches, and the like. The secondary record contains information derived from the original medical record and is used for reimbursement and research purposes. Patient financial and billing information is also generally referred to as secondary record information. It should also be noted that certain patient information (such as HIV test results and drug and alcohol abuse information) may require special treatment. These special rules will be covered later in more detail.

Content Requirements

The actual content of the patient's medical record is a matter of professional judgment. Some states have minimum content requirements for medical records, established by law; however, minimum content requirements are generally only applicable to "health care facilities" (such as hospitals, nursing homes, and ambulatory surgical centers). A well-organized, thorough record that demonstrates a specific path of care and well thought out analyses is highly advised, especially in light of the evidentiary value in malpractice and competency hearings. In addition, a thorough record should enhance your ability to effectively track and diagnose a patient's particular condition.

The patient chart is one of the most important components of the medical record. The chart details the medical history of the patient and reflects the course of action with respect to particular complaints and injuries. As previously stated, content is a matter of professional judgment. It should be noted, however, that many practitioners follow the "SOAP" method of recording patients' medical histories. SOAP stands for:

1. Subjective description
2. Objective description
3. Analysis
4. Proposed treatment

and is essentially a topical outline of what the practitioner records in his or her notes before, during, and after the office visit.

The subjective description is the patient's rendition of the injury or illness—what the patient feels, what the symptoms are, and so forth. The objective description is the findings after an examination of the patient. The analysis is just that: based on the patient's complaint and the physician's finding, what is believed to be wrong with the patient. Finally, the notes should record what action (if any) was taken to remedy the problem.

Record Storage and Retention

The physician is responsible for the records in his or her possession. Consequently, precautions must be taken to prevent theft, destruction, loss, and the inadvertent release of confidential information to unauthorized parties. The American Medical Records Association, AMRA, has published a position paper on the confidentiality of patient health information, which suggests certain guidelines health care facilities should follow with respect to medical record storage and security. Although directed toward health care facilities, the suggestions are equally helpful to any medical practitioner:

*   Records should be housed in a physically secure area under the immediate control of the health information manager (often, primary and secondary records are filed separately for purposes of convenience, though space limitations will ultimately dictate how the records are filed);
*   Access to computer files should be controlled through security

codes known only to authorized users (obvious passwords should be avoided and passwords should be changed on a regular basis);

- Areas where patient care data are maintained should be restricted to authorized personnel and not be left unattended;
- Policies and procedures should be developed that specify the method of storage for medical records along with secondary reports, logs, and files (these procedures may provide different levels of security for different types of reports and records);
- Sensitive information should be identified and tagged as such;
- Special policies and procedures should be developed to provide limited access to information that is considered sensitive, such as physician master code list, death listings and cause of death, abortions performed, and special records concerning alcohol and drug abuse patients, HIV test results, and so forth;
- All individuals who have access to the medical records should be required to sign a statement that requires them to keep all information contained in the medical record confidential. The signed statement should be kept in the employee's personnel file, independent contract file, or other appropriately labeled office file.

Following these suggestions can help to reduce the risk of loss, damage, or inadvertent release of medical records.

The practitioner should also develop a written "retention and destruction" policy. Medical records should not be retained beyond their needed use, yet it may be difficult to ascertain precisely how long that is. A retention schedule would take into account any mandatory time periods established by state law or by accrediting and/or regulatory agencies. Where none exist, AMRA suggests that a schedule be developed by answering these practical questions:

- Who will retain each type of record or data?
- What data are to be retained and in what form?
- Where are the data to be retained?
- Why are the data to be retained?
- In what format are the data to be retained?
- How long are the data to be retained?
- How will the data be destroyed?

A good starting point for developing a retention policy is to check your state's record retention requirements for health care facilities. For example, Oregon's Administrative Rules require that the following records be retained permanently in either written or computerized form:

- Patient's register (containing admissions and discharges);
- Patient's master index;
- Register of all deliveries (including live and still births);
- Register of all deaths;
- Register of all operations;
- Register of all outpatients (for seven years).

Oregon also requires that all health care facilities' medical records be kept for at least ten years after the date of the last discharge. In addition, federal regulations require records in Medicare programs to be kept for five years after the Medicare billing report is filed.

In any event, patient medical records should be retained for a relatively long period of time since they may be needed to aid in litigation, such as the defense of malpractice suits. In addition, special circumstances may require that certain records be retained even longer, such as when the physician or patient is anticipating litigation, when there is a disputed claim, or when the practitioner is subject to an open audit period. In the celebrated Dalkon Shield case, for purposes of damages, claimants were required to prove their use of the IUD through medical records that, for most, were approximately 20 years old. But generally, where a retention period is not dictated by legal requirements, development of a satisfactory retention policy is really a matter of meeting the practitioner's own needs.

When it is determined that a record is no longer needed, the practitioner should also have a specified procedure for destruction of the documents. Destruction of paper records is generally facilitated by shredding or incineration. Information stored on magnetic media is erased. Destruction or erasure should either be witnessed or attested to in writing by the individual responsible for destruction to limit potential liability for negligence in handling the medical records.

Release of Records

Several issues arise with respect to the release of a patient's medical records: specifically, who owns the record, what information is confidential, and when consent is required for release to third parties.

Ownership and Patient Access

Most states recognize that the health care provider "owns" the physical medical record, and that neither the patient nor third parties may remove the original or copies thereof, except when necessary for judicial or administrative proceedings. However, the patient is considered to have a "property right" in the record. Consequently, the patient or the patient's legal representative may request a copy; rarely is the patient entitled to the original record. Usually, the patient must sign a written authorization for the release and give "reasonable notice" of the request.

In many states, the patient's access to the record may be limited or denied where:

- The patient is a minor and is governed by legal constraints;
- The patient has been determined to be legally incompetent;
- The health care provider has determined that release of the information would be injurious to, or endanger, the patient or other persons (applicable to psychiatric information).

Some states also allow the patient's access to be limited to viewing the record or viewing or copying only a portion of it, depending on the circumstances. However, where the patient has an established legal right of access that is not specifically limited by either the circumstances or by law, denial of access may result in professional discipline and/or an award of monetary damages to the patient.

Confidentiality

Medical records contain sensitive information that is considered confidential. Confidentiality is the primary purpose for which most, if not all, record release policies are developed.

Both the Hippocratic Oath and the AMA have established a code of ethical responsibility with respect to the confidentiality of a patient's medical records. State and federal laws support this ethical responsibility by imposing penalties upon a physician who improperly discloses medical information.

State physician licensing and medical practice acts impose confidentiality obligations on practitioners in most states. Willful or negligent disclosure of confidential information can lead to a refusal to grant, or the suspension or revocation of, a license to practice.

Case law also protects the confidentiality of records under the "physician–patient privilege," and under a recognized right of privacy. Liability has been based on theories of invasion of privacy, breach of contract, breach of fiduciary duty, and malpractice, with associated penalties ranging from fines to license revocation or both. State law sometimes imposes more rigorous confidentiality requirements upon hospitals. If you are a member of a hospital's medical staff, you are subject to these same confidentiality obligations as well as those imposed on private practitioners.

Federal law protects the confidentiality of records relating to drug and alcohol abuse treatment (discussed more fully later). Improper disclosure may subject you to a fine of $500 for the first offense and up to $5000 for each additional offense.

Medicare Requirements

To help reduce the risk of inadvertent disclosure of confidential information, records that are considered "highly sensitive" should be specially marked and/or filed in separate areas to which access is restricted. Individuals who have contact with sensitive information should be educated on the importance of confidentiality and the consequences of breaching that confidentiality. Employees should sign a nondisclosure agreement contained in the employment contract, which makes improper disclosure of patient information grounds for immediate termination.

Special Confidentiality Statutes and Considerations

The federal government has promulgated special rules concerning alcohol and drug abuse patient records. The regulations cover federally assisted programs that provide alcohol or drug abuse diagnosis, treatment, or referral for treatment. The regulations specifically define what programs and records are covered, the extent of the prohibition on disclosure, exceptions to the prohibition, and the sanctions and penalties for violation of the statute.

Most states also have special rules regarding the confidentiality and disclosure of particular types of patient information. With the increasing concern over AIDS, most states have developed special confidentiality rules with respect to HIV test results. Many states also have special statutes concerning the confidentiality of mental health and developmental disability records. In addition, many states have special statutes for adoption records. These statutes, in effect, seal the court records relating to adoptions so that no one may have access to them, though a few states permit the adoptee limited access.

Maintaining confidentiality of patient information becomes an issue when the medical practice is sold or when the practice is permanently closed. When a medical practice is sold, the records are generally transferred to the new owner as part of the business. In order to facilitate a transfer that does not violate the patient's right to privacy, the patients should be notified that the practice is being transferred to a new owner who will have custody of their records. A patient may decide that he or she prefers to see a physician other than the new owner in the future. Consequently, the notice should state that, upon the patient's written request, the records will be forwarded to any practitioner specified by the patient.

When a medical practice is closed, the patients should be notified and encouraged to find a new practitioner. The notice should inform the patients that their records will be sent to their new practitioner upon their authorization. Records that are not sent to a new practitioner should not be destroyed but should be retained by the original practitioner or the practitioner's authorized custodian. Retention is preferable, since the patient may have need for the records in the future.

Finally, special consideration should be given to the confidentiality problems inherent to a computer-based record system. Today, most practices have some, if not all, of their patient information stored on computers. Since the computer has the ability to store large quantities of information, one unauthorized entry into the system can lead to the disclosure of a tremendous amount of confidential information.

Special security systems can be installed to increase the protection of confidential information. As previously noted, passwords should be used as the most basic form of protection to eliminate access to outsiders. Breaches of confidentiality are most likely to occur through the disclosure of information from an overly curious employee. Consequently, access to particularly sensitive information (such as HIV test results and drug or alcohol abuse records) should be restricted to only those who have a need and right to it. For example, the system can be installed with an alarm that sounds when an unauthorized user attempts to gain access to information beyond his or her security clearance.

As a prerequisite to granting access to the computer system, all individuals should be required to sign an agreement under which they promise to maintain the confidentiality of all medical information to which they gain access.

Necessity of Consent

In most circumstances, the release of a patient's medical information requires the patient's written authorization. Likewise, patient consent is an absolute defense to a claim of improper disclosure of confidential information. However, there must be proof of a written authorization verifying that the patient made a fully informed voluntary consent.

In order to be voluntary, the consent must be made without coercion, and the patient must have the "legal capacity" to consent. In other words, the patient must be of legal age (this varies from state to state) and of sound mind. Where the patient is a minor or is legally incompetent, the patient's parent or legal guardian must give the necessary consent for release of the information.

To ensure that the patient makes a fully informed consent, the patient must be made aware of the scope of the consent. Consequently, the authorization form should be clear and contain all of the pertinent information. The practitioner may want to consult AMRA's Model Authorization Form for Health Care Facilities for guidance. The model form suggests the inclusion of the following information:

- Name of the facility that is to release the information;
- Individual/institution that is to receive the information;
- Patient's full name, address, and date of birth;
- Reason for need of information;
- Extent or nature of information to be released;

- Specific date, event, or condition upon which authorization will expire unless revoked earlier;
- Statement that authorization can be revoked but not retroactive to the release of information made in good faith;
- Date consent is given;
- Signature of patient or legal representative.

Other important guidelines to follow include keeping the consent form with the patient's records for future reference. The information released should be strictly limited to information required to fulfill the purpose stated in the authorization. The records should be marked with the statement that the records should not be released to anyone other than the person authorized by the patient. For added protection, the practitioner may want to make the recipient sign a nondisclosure agreement.

When medical records are released to third persons, a proper authorization is normally required. Common situations where consent is necessary include insurance companies for billing purposes, other health care providers, an attorney, and a law enforcement agency (except where compelled by law). Upon the death of patients, their medical records may be obtained and/or released only by consent of their legal representatives.

There are also situations where the patient's consent is not required for release of medical information. Certain information is simply not considered privileged and is, therefore, subject to release without consent. Nonprivileged information includes such items as the patient's name, sex, and city of residence.

The most common situation where consent is not required is when a medical emergency necessitates release to another health care provider and the patient or legal representative is unable to give consent. The subsequent provider will be under the same duty to keep the information confidential; confidentiality is not waived when the records are transferred.

Consent is not necessary where the law mandates disclosure of certain medical information. In most states, there are certain types of information that must be reported to specific public agencies. Several examples of the many different types of information that may be required to be reported include confirmed cases of AIDS and other communicable diseases, instances of child or elder abuse and rape, unusual deaths, and workers' compensation claim information. The reporting requirements vary from state to state as to what types of cases must be reported and the manner and extent of the reports that must be filed. The practitioner who complies with the reporting requirements is granted immunity from any liability for disclosing the information.

In many states, consent may not be required for the release of information to local authorities where the patient presents an immediate danger to himself or another person. The practitioner must use professional judgment as to when the threat is serious enough to warrant disclosure. However, it should be noted that courts in many states have imposed a special duty on practitioners who deal with dangerous psychiatric patients to actually breach confidentiality, following a ruling from a California court that held that a practitioner may be found civilly liable for the death of another when the practitioner knows of a patient's intention to kill a particular person and the practitioner fails to disclose the danger to the intended victim and/or local authorities.

Other situations where consent is usually not required include release of information to government payors such as Medicare or Medicaid (when necessary to secure compensation for services rendered), in response to a subpoena, and disclosure to the parents of a minor for treatment rendered to the minor.

State law plays a major role with respect to many of the issues that are pertinent to medical record retention, release, and confidentiality. In light of the practitioner's legal and ethical responsibility toward patients, and the consequent civil liability that flows from an improper disclosure, the practitioner should check with an attorney or the local chapter of their professional association for further information on confidentiality and the release and retention of medical records in general.

13

Bookkeeping and Accounting

Business Records

Accounting

The purpose of any accounting system is to keep accurate records of the financial condition of the practice. A well-organized accounting system that is amenable to analysis can make encounters with the IRS less traumatic. In addition, when it becomes necessary to borrow money, creditors will look more favorably upon a professional who maintains complete records that accurately reflect the practice's fiscal condition.

Devising a satisfactory accounting system can be a rather arduous task. Although medical practitioners have considerable latitude in designing their accounting system, their freedom in this matter is not absolute. Constraints are imposed by various state and federal laws, such as tax laws, and by the Financial Accounting Standards Board of the American Institute of Certified Public Accountants (AICPA), in its regulations known as "generally accepted accounting principles (GAAP)." The law in this area, especially the federal tax laws, are in a constant state of flux. In addition, it may be desirable to establish within the accounting system the necessary records to meet the needs of the practice, both for tax purposes and for business purposes.

In light of these observations and the simple fact that most health care professionals lack any formal accounting training or experience, it will be assumed that the practitioner will hire a professional accountant to set up and maintain an accounting system. Therefore, this discussion will merely provide an introduction to some of the basic issues and terminology pertaining to accounting procedures to prepare you to ask the right questions and make well-informed decisions when you meet with your accountant.

Business Year

Accounting data may be arranged into monthly, quarterly, or yearly statements. Business years may be measured according to a calendar year or a fiscal year. If an organization adopts the calendar year, its business year will begin on January 1 and end on December 31. The calendar year is convenient because it corresponds to the normal time reference. Individuals, partners, and service corporations must adopt a calendar year for tax reporting. If an organization adopts the fiscal year, its business year will begin and end on the date it chooses. The fiscal year is more suitable for businesses that are engaged in seasonal activity because it allows the organization the flexibility to meet its own particular timing needs. It may also be more desirable for medical professionals who do not maintain a full-time private practice but whose primary occupation is teaching.

Cash and Accrual Bookkeeping Methods

There are essentially two methods of recording income and expenses on the books: cash and accrual. In the cash method of accounting, all actual receipts and expenditures during a given accounting period are recorded for that period. If the practice receives and pays a $10,000 bill in year one, it would record both the receipt and expense of $10,000 in year one. The cash method is the one preferred by most service-oriented businesses such as health care professionals, since there are usually substantial amounts of receivables that might result in tax liability under the accrual method, discussed below.

The accrual method, on the other hand, employs a fiction to determine receipts and expenditures in an attempt to match the income a practice receives to the expenses incurred in generating that income. Costs and expenses are recorded as they accrue, or are incurred, rather than at the time of cash payment. Income is recognized as it is accrued, or earned, and not at the time of collection. For example, if a practice pays $10,000 for a new piece of lab equipment in year one but does not install and use the equipment until year two, the $10,000 expense would not be recorded in year one at all. Instead, the $10,000 would be at least partially recorded in year two if use of the equipment produced income for that year.

The accrual basis results in financial statements that recognize transactions and directly related costs at the time the transaction occurs, and other income and expenses in the period in which they accrue or are incurred and not necessarily when cash changes hands. Thus a surgeon using the accrual method would record the receivable for an operation performed on the date of surgery rather than the date when payment is received. The accrual method is designed to present the fairest picture of the results of a profit-making enterprise and is thus widely used. The cash basis has the advantage of simplicity, but rarely provides a fair representation of the results of operations, because the deduction of all expenses in the year they are paid, regardless of earnings, does not accurately match expenses with income.

Current and Capital Expenditures

The choice between the two aforementioned bookkeeping methods is not entirely left to the discretion of the taxpayer. By law, "capital expenses" must be allocated over a number of years, which in effect imposes an accrual method. Many of the expenditures necessary to maintain a health care practice are capital, as opposed to "current expenses."

Whether an expense is identified as a capital or a current expense depends on the length of the useful life of the asset. If an item purchased is to be consumed or used up in the current accounting period (usually one year), it is characterized as a current expense for that year. Wooden tongue depressors and fluoride rinse are examples of current expenses.

If the life of the asset extends into future accounting periods, its cost is a capital expense and must be spread over the useful life of the asset. For example, an X-ray machine would be amortized for the useful life of the machine, and a prepaid insurance premium would be amortized for the length of the policy. This means that the cost of the item must be evenly spread over the number of years the item is expected to be in service.

Depreciation is the method by which the cost of a capital asset is recovered through yearly deductions. In theory, a capital asset is consumed over its useful life; thus the business is permitted to deduct for tax purposes a portion of the cost of the item for each year of the item's useful life. There is at least one exception to the depreciation rule found in the code. The purchaser may elect to deduct up to $10,000 of the cost of a capital asset for the year it is purchased and put into use.

Depreciation is limited to those assets that physically lose value over time. Depreciable property includes equipment, buildings, machinery, and vehicles used in business or held for production of income. An expenditure of $50,000 on lab equipment is recorded as a capital expense (as opposed to a current expense) because the expenditure will provide benefit in future years and thus should not be charged as an expense in the year purchased. However, such an asset, like most tangible fixed assets other than land, will not last forever; ultimately, it will have to be retired because it is physically worn out or has become inefficient or obsolete.

The method of depreciation is dependent upon when the asset was placed into service. There are numerous methods of depreciation, each of which can produce markedly different results.

Most assets placed in service after 1980 and prior to 1987 are covered by a depreciation system called Accelerated Cost Recovery System (ACRS); for items put in service from 1987 to date the depreciation system is called the Modified Accelerated Cost Recovery System (MACRS). The cost of an item of depreciable property is generally recoverable over a 3 to 3½-year period, depending into which one of certain specified classes it falls. For example, office furniture and equipment is considered "five-year property," for which a statutory percentage is applied to the unadjusted cost of the property to determine the recovery deduction for each year.

An issue related to depreciation calculation is whether expenditures relating to a depreciable asset, such as improvements or repairs, should be treated as current expenses or whether they should be capitalized and added to the basis (cost) of the asset. Generally, if repairs or improvements arrest deterioration and appreciably prolong the life of the asset, the expenditure should be capitalized. If the expenditure involves only a minor repair, it should be treated as a current expense. In borderline cases, the decision may rest upon the tax advantage. (See Chapter 14.)

Investment Tax Credit

Depreciation deductions reduce the tax burden by being subtracted from the taxpayer's gross income to determine taxable income. Deductions do not result in dollar-for-dollar tax savings, that is, one dollar of deductions will not reduce taxes by one dollar. One dollar of tax credit, however, will reduce taxes by one dollar because credits are subtracted directly from the tax liability after the tax rates have been applied.

For the businessperson, the most significant credit is the investment tax credit (ITC). The ITC was initially established to encourage private investment in old and new businesses by offering a credit on certain investment properties.

Financial Statements

Financial statements report on the status and activities of a business. They take many forms. At a minimum, a business will need an income statement, a balance sheet, and, possibly, a statement of owner's equity.

1. *Income Statement*   The income statement is known by various names. It may be called a profit-and-loss statement, report on earnings, operating statement, or simply income statement. This statement reports the income that has been earned, the costs or expenses that have been incurred, and the net profit. It shows what has taken place in the business, from a financial standpoint, over a given accounting period.

From the various entries that comprise the statement, financial ratios can be derived. By comparing income statements to one another over several years, trends and patterns can be identified. Comparison of these income statements may infuse new meaning into the present income statement; that is, the impact of a single income statement on an observer is likely to be less important when it is considered in context. For instance, when this year's income statement discloses a lower profit margin, that may merely mean that more money was spent on new lab equipment, and future years' earnings will consequently go up. Therefore, the slight dip in profit will be less alarming.

2. *Balance Sheet* Unlike the income statement, which reflects the financial condition of a business over an accounting period, the balance sheet indicates the financial position of the business at a given moment. The income statement reflects the way things were; the balance sheet reflects the way things are.

Balance sheets are composed of three basic elements: assets, liabilities, and owner's equity. For the sheet to balance (and the business considered solvent), assets must be equal to liabilities plus owner's equity.

(i) *Assets.* Assets are categorized as either current assets or long-term (fixed) assets. Current assets are defined as assets that are likely to be consumed or subjected to change (usually converted into cash) within one year. Current assets also include any portion of a long-term asset that may be realized within one year. Cash, accounts receivable (if collectible within one year of the statement), investments, and inventory are examples of current assets.

Long-term assets are assets used to operate a business but are not for resale, for example, an examining table. A given asset may be either current or long-term, depending on its particular use in a given business. Long-term assets may be either tangible or intangible.

Tangible long-term assets include property (land and office space) and equipment. These assets are usually valued at cost less allowed depreciation, where cost includes both the purchase price and any expense incurred in preparing the asset for use (for example, the cost of installing and testing a new X-ray machine).

Intangible long-term assets include such things as goodwill (if purchased as part of the business) and any patent, trademark, or copyright the practitioner may own. Goodwill is potentially the most valuable of intangible assets. Goodwill is the value of an active practice and includes the organization, trained staff, business reputation, established patients, and location, and can include lists of patients, long-term leases, and contracts. Goodwill is what makes a business sell for more than the aggregate value of its tangible assets. Goodwill cannot be recorded on the books unless one pays for it in the purchase of a practice.

(ii) *Liabilities.* Liabilities are also divided into current and long-term. Current liabilities are obligations due within one year. Any portion of a long-term liability that is due within one year is deemed a current liability. Current liabilities also include accounts payable (to outsiders as well as salaries to personnel), payroll taxes and benefits, accrued income taxes, and other accrued liabilities (such as short-term notes).

Long-term liabilities are obligations having a maturity date a year or more beyond the present accounting period. Long-term liabilities include mortgages, notes payable, and accounts payable.

(iii) *Owner's Equity*. Owner's equity plus liabilities equals assets, or, said in another way, equity equals assets minus liabilities. Owner's equity reflects the net worth of the business. Generally, the larger the owner's equity, the more there is available to the owner for distribution or liquidation. However, the amounts reported as owner's equity do not necessarily reveal the amounts that can reasonably be withdrawn. For the health care professional, most assets are in the form of fixed assets, such as lab/office equipment and buildings/property, and a withdrawal of these assets would be impractical or impossible. Thus there are certain practical and legal limitations to the amount of money that may be distributed to the owners from the owner's equity account.

It often becomes necessary or desirable to establish a reserve account. Such an account may be required by law or may be established voluntarily. Reserve accounts, which diminish the amount of owner's equity available for distribution or other use, may be created for acquisition, to meet contingent liabilities, such as pending lawsuits or taxes, or to increase the capital structure of the practice.

From a creditor's viewpoint, the owner's equity represents the amount a practice can lose before the creditor's interests become jeopardized. Therefore, creditors will look to the owner's equity account to ensure that their interests are being protected by a capital cushion.

Given the importance of the owner's equity, it may be desirable to account for it in a separate financial statement, particularly if the owner's equity is composed of several entries or is constantly fluctuating. An owner's equity statement should report the amount of the owner's equity at the beginning of the accounting period, the various increases and decreases that took place during the period, and the amount of the owner's equity at the end of the period.

Intangible Business Characteristics

Income statements, balance sheets, and owner's equity statements present a financial picture of the practice, but they do not necessarily present the total picture. Two businesses having identical financial statements may have very different future prospects because of the various intangible characteristics of each one. If a practice is being examined by outsiders (such as possible lenders or purchasers of the practice), it is advantageous to include a description of these intangibles, particularly if favorable, as a part of the total financial report. A health care professional, for example, would want to report upon the established patient base, the quality of the trained staff and reputation of the licensed professionals, the positive relationship between the practice and its patients, location, and so forth.

Sources of Information on Accounting

Some of the major topics of accounting procedure have been discussed here. However, the daily mechanics of the accounting process have not been considered. For this information, the health care professional can refer to various self-help bookkeeping and accounting texts, but should ultimately consult with a Certified Public Accountant experienced in dealing with comparable practices.

14

Taxing Considerations

After allowing for basic needs through personal exemptions, a narrow list of personal deductions, and one reduced tax rate at the low end of the income scale, our income tax system is essentially a fixed-rate system. The 1990 income tax amendments to the Internal Revenue Code (IRC) added an additional rate increment that roughly separates moderate-income from high-income individuals. This created three graduated tax rates for individuals: 15 percent on the lowest taxable income range, 28 percent on income in the middle taxable range, and 31 percent on income in the highest taxable income range. In addition, as of 1991, a modest capital gains preference was reinstated. As a result, long-term capital gains are taxed at 28 percent; therefore, high-income individuals will receive a 3 percent tax reduction on certain income (i.e., capital gains), which would ordinarily be taxed at 31 percent. (The capital gains tax will be discussed in detail later in this chapter.) Thus, with the exception of the capital gains preference, individuals earning more money are still taxed at a higher overall rate. In other respects, however, higher and lower incomes are treated alike by the Internal Revenue Service (IRS).

Due to the immensity of the IRC and the frequency with which it changes, it would be impossible to address all of the pertinent issues in any detail in this book. It is hoped that the reader will consult a competent professional tax adviser before implementing any tax-affected operations. This chapter is presented to give the reader sufficient familiarity with the tax issues to be able to discuss them with advisers and associates.

Of primary importance are the tax consequences that result from the choice of one business form over another—not as dramatic today as ten years ago but still important. In addition, it is important to understand the tax aspects of employee compensation and benefits. Finally, the proper use of income spreading, deductions, and the recently reinstated capital gains preference will be explained, to shed some light on ways that you can effectively reduce your overall tax liability.

The Tax Consequences of Business Organization

Prior to the 1986 Tax Reform Act, beneficial tax treatment was the primary impetus behind many professionals' choice to incorporate rather than creating a partnership or remaining sole proprietors. Individual tax rates were as high as 70 percent, while the top corporate rate was around 34 percent—a major tax shelter for those who were able to incorporate. The 1986 Act reduced individual rates to levels equal or below corporate rates.

Four years earlier, the Tax Equity and Fiscal Responsibility Act (TEFRA) took away one of the other primary advantages of incorporation. Prior to this Act, corporate shareholders benefited from the ability to invest a greater amount of income in tax-deferred retirement plans than persons in partnerships or sole proprietorships could. TEFRA, in effect, leveled the playing field so that the choice of business form would not be influenced by variations in tax treatment of retirement plans.

Although the tax benefits of the various business organizations have been roughly equalized, there are still some differences with respect to the tax treatment of the various entities.

1. *Sole Proprietorships*

As with S corporations and partnerships, a sole proprietorship's income and deductions pass through to the sole proprietor and are reported on his or her individual income tax return. Even though the business form is labeled sole proprietorship, the practitioner may employ several other practitioners on a salaried basis without affecting his or her personal tax treatment.

2. *Partnerships*

Partnerships are taxed in much the same way as S corporations—business income (and deductions) pass directly through to the individual partners. With certain exceptions, each partner's distributable share is taxed at his or her individual income tax rate. There are, however, more technical rules that apply to different situations. Since partnership tax is a very complicated body of law, if you choose this business form it is recommended that you consult with an accountant.

3. *Corporations*

As was discussed in Chapter 1, there are two types of corporations—the C corporation and the S corporation. The designation "professional corporation" does not affect the tax characterization. The professional C corporation is regarded as a separate legal entity. Therefore, it is taxed as a separate entity. All corporate income is taxed at the corporate rate (34 percent for professional service corporations as of the date of this writing), and then again at the shareholder level when it is distributed as dividends. One might think that this shareholder-level tax could be avoided, or at least postponed, by causing the corporation to retain its earnings instead of paying them out. But Congress has dealt with this possible abuse through the imposition of an "accumulated earnings tax."

The accumulated earnings tax is a 28 percent "penalty tax" that is imposed on all accumulated earnings—earnings the IRS treats as dividends that should have been distributed. Accumulated earnings are defined as earnings in excess of reasonable business needs. If the accumulation can be justified (for example, to allow for an anticipated and legitimate expansion of your business), the tax likely will not be imposed. There are additional ways to avoid this tax that should be discussed with your tax adviser if you perceive the possibility of liability.

It is this "two-tier" tax—once at the corporate level and again at the shareholder level—that dissuades many small businesses from opting for C corporation status. There are methods of reducing the shareholder tax using the maximum allowable deductions (as will be discussed later in this chapter). Most small businesses elect to be treated as an S corporation and thereby eliminate the potential double tax.

In order to be taxed as an S corporation, a special election must be made and filed with the IRS. In addition, certain requirements must be met: There may be no more than 35 shareholders; there may not be shareholders who are "nonindividuals" (except certain estates and trusts), such as another corporation; there may not be nonresident aliens as shareholders; and the corporation may not have more than one class of stock.

S corporations avoid double taxation because corporate income passes through directly to the shareholders. There is no trap of corporate earnings at the corporate level. Each shareholder must recognize a proportionate amount of corporate income directly on his or her individual income tax return, which is taxed at individual income tax rates. That means a tax savings of three percent for individuals in the highest income bracket (assuming a flat corporate rate of 34 percent and individual rate of 31 percent). However, the tax savings may be nonexistent when consideration is given to state income tax rates at both the corporate level and the individual level. Most of the standard business deductions that are applicable to the C corporation are also applicable to the S corporation. The shareholders utilize the business deductions themselves, in proportion to their ownership. Such deductions can, however, be used only to offset business profits, not unrelated income.

Employee Compensation and Benefits

1. *Employee Compensation*

For practitioners who have chosen to do business as C corporations, payment of employee compensation is actually one of the most effective ways to minimize or eliminate double taxation. Rather than paying out corporate earnings to stockholder-employees as nondeductible dividends, the corporation can pay out high salaries and then receive a business expense deduction for the wages paid.

Although an S corporation is not saddled with the double tax, the corporation (shareholders) still benefits from a deduction for employee compensation, since it results in a decrease in taxable income.

It should be apparent that this deduction provides a potentially large loophole in the IRC. Congress and the courts have all but closed this loophole by placing a limit on the amount that may be deducted as a business expense—only that which is "reasonable compensation" may be deducted.

A corporation cannot avoid income tax by paying excessive salaries to the stockholder-employees. The IRS frequently audits closely held corporations for this type of abuse. Although most challenges are to salaries and benefits for stockholders, excessive compensation paid to a nonstockholder-employee also has been successfully challenged by the IRS.

Reasonableness, as always, depends on all the circumstances of the particular case. Factors that the courts have considered include the nature of the job, the size and complexity of the business, prevailing rates of compensation, the company's profitability, the uniqueness of the employee's skills or experience, the number of hours worked, the employee's salary as compared with the salaries of coworkers, general economic conditions, and the presence, absence, and amount of dividends paid.

If a salary is found excessive, no deduction will be allowed for the part of the payment that is excessive. Even though the employer cannot deduct the full amount paid, the employee must report and pay tax on the full amount received.

Usually, a new business is more concerned with underpayment than overcompensation. Employees may work long, hard hours with little compensation in the hope of a brighter future. The IRS realizes this. In later years, when the business is profitable, employees can be compensated for the underpayment of former years by additions to their salaries. The base salaries must be reasonable and the additional amounts also must be reasonable in light of the past services performed and the compensation already received.

Compensation also may be fixed as a percentage of profits or earnings. Contingent plans of this nature may result in low salaries in lean years and above-average salaries in good years. The IRS accepts this too, so long as, on the average, the salaries are not unreasonable. Of course, some premium is reasonable due to the risk assumed by the employee who accepts such a plan.

Contingent plans are suspect, however, when used for owner-employees since they can be used to avoid dividends in good years. A stockholder-employee's reward for an increase in business should be a reasonable salary and increased dividends.

2. Benefit Plans

Statutory, tax-exempt benefit plans are available for accident and health coverage, group term life insurance, profit sharing, pension, and contributory savings plans, to name a few. These plans are not limited to corporate employers. The requirements for benefit plans are extremely complex from a tax standpoint, and retirement plans must also comply with ERISA, the federal Employee Retirement Income Security Act.

Even though the myriad rules and regulations are tedious, the plans are worth consideration. If a plan conforms to the rules, employer contributions are immediately deductible as business expenses but are not taxable to the employees as income. Employees are taxed only when they receive payments from the plan. Even more important, in the case of retirement plans no tax is imposed on the investment growth of funds deposited in the plan.

Statutory Benefit Plans Statutory benefit plans can provide accident, medical, or group term life insurance, educational assistance, legal services, or child care. Each is covered by separate rules and requirements, but all plans must meet a common set of rules to be tax-exempt.

Generally, structuring plans to favor highly compensated employees will subject the employees to tax liability on those benefits. This is a complex area and you should consult with your tax adviser or accountant before adopting any of these plans.

A statutory plan also must meet a benefits requirement so that the average benefit received by non-highly compensated employees must equal or exceed 75 percent of the average benefits received by highly compensated employees under the same or similar plans.

A highly compensated employee is an employee who owns 5 percent of the business, or receives compensation in excess of $75,000 annually, or receives over $50,000 and is in the highest paid group of employees for the year, or is an officer and receives more than $45,000 in compensation annually. These numbers are in effect as of the date of this writing but are indexed annually to reflect inflation.

In determining the required eligibility percentages, the following employees may be excluded: temporary and part-time employees, employees who are under 21 years old, employees covered by collective bargaining agreements (unions), employees who are nonresident aliens and who receive no U.S. taxable income, and employees who have been on the job less than one year (six months in the case of medical benefits).

Following is a sketchy review of some statutory plans:

- An employer may provide up to $50,000 of tax-free, group term life insurance for each employee. Premiums on coverage exceeding $50,000 in face amount are taxable to employees, unless the employee contributes to the plan with his or her own taxable income.
- An employee may receive up to $5,250 in tax-free educational assistance per year from a funded educational assistance program.

In addition, contributions by employers to health and accident plans are generally tax-exempt during the term of employment only if they provide continuing extensions of coverage for various specified time periods after termination of employment.

When an employee receives payment for medical expenses, the amount received is not taxable income unless the employee is already receiving compensation from another source or takes an income tax deduction for the medical expenses.

The employee is also not taxed on amounts received to compensate for injury due to permanent loss of use of a body part or function or permanent disfigurement.

Amounts received to compensate an employee for loss of income due to illness or injury are taxable as income.

A plan can provide assistance for child or other dependent care. The aggregate amount excluded from the employee's income cannot exceed $5000 in the case of a single parent or marital unit. If an employee receives $2500 of tax-free child care assistance, the spouse is eligible to receive only an additional $2500 in tax-free assistance.

Qualified Plans Retirement benefits may be provided under "Qualified Plans." The rules for qualified pension, profit sharing, and stock bonus plans are too numerous to summarize.

Eligibility and benefit rules exist to ensure nondiscrimination. Since it is reasonable to allow for different employer contribution amounts to various plans based on an employee's value and years of service, there are special rules to prevent and remedy top-heavy plans where accumulated contributions on behalf of highly compensated employees exceed those for other employees.

These plans must be separately funded and administered under rules designed to guarantee, to the extent possible, that retirement funds cannot be reached, tampered with, squandered, or mismanaged by the employer.

There are also vesting requirements so that employees can rely on the plans without worrying about forfeiture due to excessively long employment period requirements. Maintenance of a qualified plan is impossible without specialized professional help.

Cafeteria Plans "Cafeteria plans" have nothing to do with employee lunchrooms. Under a cafeteria plan, an employer may set up a "menu" whereby an employee is allotted a certain amount of benefit credit and allowed to choose between various amounts and combinations of plans or the receipt of additional taxable income. Amounts allocable to elected benefit plans are not taxable to the employee. In this way, an employee can tailor a benefits program to best meet his or her individual circumstances. Fringe benefits and educational assistance plans may not be included in cafeteria plans.

Fringe Benefits Certain fringe benefits may be provided tax-free to employees. Such benefits might include employee discounts, subsidized cafeterias, parking facilities, onsite athletic facilities, and so forth. Generally, these benefits must be of no additional cost to the employer, or be worth so little that the administrative cost of keeping track of them exceeds the value of the benefit.

Shareholder employees of C corporations can take advantage of all of the above fringe benefits as employees. S corporation shareholders generally cannot avail themselves of certain fringe benefits such as cafeteria plans, fully deductible health insurance at the corporate level, dependent care plans, or group term life plans.

Keeping Taxes Low

There are two primary means of reducing tax liability. One is to spread taxable income out over time and thereby defer tax payment. The other way is to use the maximum possible deductions to reduce net taxable income.

Income Spreading through Installments and Deferred Payments

One way you can spread income is to receive it in installments. If you are using the cash method of accounting, you will not be taxed until you actually receive payment. (For a full discussion of the cash and accrual methods of accounting, see Chapter 13.) By spreading income through deferred payments, you do not actually avoid taxes (since each installment is taxed), but you may be able to pay less tax overall.

The best way to understand how deferred payment works is through an illustration. Suppose you provide services for a total of $80,000 in year one. If you did not use a deferred payment plan, you would be taxed at the maximum rate in year one. If, instead, you work out a payment plan with the patient to pay $20,000 a year (plus interest), you have only $20,000 of income to report per year. If you were to have little or no other income during the four years of repayment, you may be in a lower tax bracket than if you took receipt of the full $80,000 in one year. Consequently, you pay less tax overall.

Of course, there is the risk that the patient may never repay you in full, so the deferred payment schedule will not be suitable in all instances. In addition, in order to use the cash method, certain requirements must be met if your practice is a C corporation. The corporation must be a "qualified personal service corporation," which means that the corporation must be "substantially engaged" in the activity of providing (health) services. If the corporation were also actively involved in real estate development, for example, it might not qualify for the cash method of accounting. A corporation that does not meet the qualified personal service corporation exception may still qualify for the cash method if its gross receipts do not exceed an average of $5,000,000 per year over the three years prior to the year in which the corporation elects to use the cash method.

Spreading Income among Family Members

Another strategy for business owners in high tax brackets is to divert some income directly to members of their immediate families who are in lower tax brackets by hiring them as employees. Putting dependent children on the payroll can result in a substantial tax savings because their salaries can be deducted as a business expense, but, at the same time, you may not be required to withhold Social Security from the children's wages.

Your child can earn up to the amount of the standard deduction without any tax liability, which, as of the date of this writing, is $3600. In addition, there is an exemption of $2300, provided that the child cannot be claimed as a dependent. This is a potential total of $5900. You, as the taxpayer, can still claim a personal dependency exemption for the child if you provide over half of his or her support; however, the amount the child could earn without any tax liability would drop to $3400. This salary arrangement is permissible so long as the child is under 19 years of age or, if 19 or older, is a full-time student. The following are other restrictions on such an arrangement:

1. The salary must be reasonable in relation to the child's age and the work performed.
2. The work performed must be a necessary service to the business.
3. The work must actually be performed by the child.

Proper Use of Deductions

If deductions are used properly, net taxable income can be reduced to zero in some instances. There are several major deductions that a business may use. You must keep full and accurate records of your expenses in case a deduction is ever challenged. Receipts are a necessity. Even if your practice is home-based, you should have a separate checking account and a complete set of books for all of the activities of your practice.

1. *Business Expenses.* Many of the daily expenditures a practice incurs are deductible from income. Current expenses are items with a useful life of less than one year. Writing utensils and stationery, postage, cotton balls, and tongue depressors are all examples of current expenses. Continuing education expenses are also generally deductible as current expenses.

Many expenses, however, cannot be fully deducted in the year of purchase but must be depreciated. These kinds of costs are called *capital expenditures.* For example, the costs of equipment such as a computer, X-ray equipment, or office furniture, all of which have useful lives of more than one year, are capital expenditures and cannot be fully deducted in the year of purchase. Instead, the taxpayer must depreciate, or allocate, the cost of the item over the estimated useful life of the asset. Although the actual useful life of professional equipment will vary, fixed periods have been established in the IRC over which depreciation may be deducted. (See Chapter 13.)

In some cases, it may be difficult to decide whether an expense is a capital expenditure or a current expense. Repairs to machinery are one example. If you spend $200 repairing lab equipment, this expense may or may not constitute a capital expenditure. The general test is whether the amount spent restoring the equipment adds to its value or substantially prolongs its useful life. Since the cost of replacing short-lived parts to keep it in efficient working condition does not substantially add to its useful life, such a cost would be a current cost and would be deductible. The cost of rebuilding the equipment, on the other hand, significantly extends its useful life. Such a cost is a capital expenditure and must be depreciated.

For many small businesses, an immediate deduction can be taken when equipment is purchased. Up to $10,000 of such purchases may be "expensed" each year and need not be depreciated at all.

Fees paid to lawyers or accountants for business purposes are generally deductible as current expenses. The same is true of salaries paid to others whose services are necessary for business. If you need to hire help, it may be advantageous to hire people on an individual-project basis as independent contractors rather than as regular employees. This avoids your having to pay Social Security, disability, and withholding tax payments on their account. You should specify the job-by-job basis of the assignments, detail when each project is to be completed, and, if possible, allow the person you are hiring to choose the place to do the work. There may be other restrictions on characterizing an individual as an independent contractor; you should discuss this with your attorney or tax adviser.

Employee Compensation As was already discussed, employee compensation deductions are very useful for the practice in which most of the employees are shareholders.

Business Use of an Automobile If you or your employees use personal vehicles for business, an amount proportionate with the business use may qualify for depreciation, maintenance, and operating expense deductions. You must keep accurate records of the number of "business miles" driven, and of the time, place, and purpose of the travel. If records are not kept, no deduction will be allowed. The records must establish total annual mileage, commuting mileage, business mileage, percentage of business use, and the date the vehicle was placed in service. This information must be reported on the tax return. You will also be asked to indicate whether there is written evidence to support the claimed use of the vehicle for business. If the vehicle is a "luxury" vehicle, there are special rules that apply for depreciation purposes.

If an automobile is used solely for business, records separating business from personal use are not necessary if certain conditions are met: (1) the vehicle is leased or owned by the employer and provided to one or more employees for use in connection with the business; (2) the vehicle is kept at the employer's premises when not in use and no employee using the vehicle lives at the employer's address; and (3) a written policy of the employer forbids personal use of the vehicle, and the vehicle is not used personally except for minor deviations such as lunch stops while on the road for business purposes.

Travel Expenses On a business trip, whether within the United States or abroad, your ordinary and necessary expenses, including travel and lodging, may be 100 percent deductible if your travel is solely for business purposes, except for luxury water travel. Business meals and meals consumed while on a business trip are deductible up to 80 percent of the actual cost. If the trip primarily involves a personal vacation, you can deduct business-related expenses at the destination, but you may not deduct the transportation costs.

If the trip is primarily for business, but part of the time is given to a personal vacation, you must indicate which expenses are for business and which are for pleasure. This is not true in the case of foreign trips if one of the following exceptions applies:

- You had no control over arranging the trip;
- The trip outside of the United States was for a week or less;
- You are not a managing executive or shareholder of the company that employed you.

If you are claiming one of these exceptions, you should be careful to have supporting documentation. If you cannot take advantage of one of the exceptions, you must allocate expenses for the trip abroad according to the percentage of the trip devoted to business (as opposed to vacation).

The definition of what constitutes a "business day" can be very helpful to the taxpayer in determining a trip's deductibility. Travel days, including the day of departure and the day of return, count as business days if travel outside the United States is for more than seven days and business activities occurred on such days. Any day that the taxpayer spends on business counts as a business day even if only a part of the day is spent on business. A day in which business is canceled through no fault of the taxpayer counts as a business day. Saturdays, Sundays, and holidays count as business days even though no business is conducted, provided that business is conducted on the Friday before and the Monday after the weekend, or on one day on either side of the holiday.

Entertainment Expenses Entertainment expenses incurred for the purpose of developing an existing practice are also deductible in the amount of 80 percent of actual cost. You must, however, be especially careful about recording entertainment expenses. You should record in your log book the amount, date, place, type of entertainment, business purpose, substance and length of the discussion, the participants in the discussion, and the business relationship of the parties who are being entertained. Keep receipts for any expenses over $25. You should also keep in mind the new stipulation in the IRC that disallows deductibility for expenses that are "lavish or extravagant under the circumstances." No guidelines have yet been developed as to the definition of the term "lavish or extravagant," but one should be aware of the restriction nevertheless. If tickets to a sporting, cultural, or other entertainment event are purchased, only the face value of the ticket is allowed as a deduction. If tickets to a sporting, cultural, or other entertainment event are purchased, only the face value of the ticket is allowed as a deduction, subject to the 20 percent reduction and further subject to the rules regarding substantiation of the business purpose. If a skybox or other luxury box seat is purchased or leased and is used for business entertaining, the maximum deduction now allowed is the cost of a nonluxury box seat.

Expenses the IRS Scrutinizes The above rules cover business travel and entertainment expenses both inside and outside of the United States. The rules are more stringent for expenses incurred while attending conventions and conferences outside the United States. Also, the IRS tends to review very carefully any deductions for attendance at seminars that also involve a family vacation, whether inside the United States or abroad. In order to deduct the expense, the taxpayer must be able to show, with documents, that the reason for attending the meeting was to promote production of income. Normally, for a spouse's expenses to be deductible, the spouse's presence must be required by the employer. In the case of an independent practitioner who has organized into a partnership or small corporation, it is wise to make the spouse a partner, employee, or member of the board of the corporation. Often, seminars will offer special activities for husbands and wives that will provide documentation later on.

As a general rule, the business deductions are allowed for conventions and seminars held in North America. The IRS is taking a closer look at cruise ship seminars and is now requiring two statements to be attached to the tax return. The first statement substantiates the number of days on the ship, the number of hours spent each day on business, and the activities in the program. The second statement must come from the sponsor of the convention to verify the first information. In addition, the ship must be registered in the United States, and all ports of call must be located in the United States or its possessions. Again, the key for the taxpayer taking this sort of deduction is careful documentation and substantiation.

What Goes into a Log Book   Keeping a log book or expense diary is probably the best line of defense for the practitioner with respect to business expenses incurred while traveling. If you are on the road, keep in mind the things in the lists that follow.

With respect to travel expenses:

- Keep proof of the costs;
- Record the time of departure;
- Record the number of days spent on business;
- List the places visited and the business purposes of your activities.

With respect to the transportation costs:

- Keep copies of all receipts in excess of $25, and if traveling by car, keep track of mileage;
- Log all other expenses in your diary.

Similarly, with meals, tips, and lodging, keep receipts for all items over $25 and make sure to record all less expensive items in your log book.

Practitioners may also obtain tax deductions for their attendance at workshops, seminars, retreats, and the like, provided they are careful to document the business nature of the trip. Accurate recordkeeping is the first line of defense for tax preparation. Note that it is no longer possible to deduct for investment seminars or conventions (as opposed to business conventions).

Deductions for Use of a Home in Business   One of the most significant and problematic of the business deductions is the workspace, or "home office," deduction. It is not uncommon for smaller practices to be based fully or partially at home for a variety of reasons, the most common of which is probably economic. The cost of renting a separate office is such that many small-practice owners, especially in the startup phase, are unwilling or unable to pay for it. Others, of course, choose to work at home because it enables them to juggle work and family. Whatever the reason, practitioners who wish to claim deductions for use of their homes in their practices will have to do some careful planning.

For some time, the IRS did not allow deductions for offices or studios in homes. This policy was challenged in a case in which a physician managed rental properties as a sideline. The doctor's rental business was run out of an office in his house, and the space was used only for this particular business. When the physician deducted the expenses for the office in his home, the IRS disallowed the deduction. However, the court was apparently convinced by the physical setup of the room that the doctor used it exclusively and regularly as an office in connection with his rental business. The court noted that the room had no television set, sofa, or bed.

This decision now has been incorporated into the IRC. As a general rule, a business deduction is not allowed for the use of a dwelling that is used as a residence by the taxpayer during the taxable year. Use as a residence is defined as the use of the unit for personal purposes for more than 14 days of the taxable year. The tax code makes an exception to this general rule in certain circumstances, allowing the taxpayer to take a deduction for a portion of a dwelling unit "exclusively used on a regular basis . . . as a principal place of business for any trade or business of the taxpayer," even if that business is not the taxpayer's primary source of income.

Exclusive and Regular Use The exclusive and regular use exception applies to any portion of the residence used exclusively and on a regular basis as the owner's principal place of conducting that business.

The qualifications for this exception are strictly construed by the IRS and the courts. The requirement of exclusivity means that the taxpayer may not mix personal use and business use. In other words, an office that doubles as a storeroom for personal belongings, a laundry room, guest bedroom, or the like will not qualify as an office for tax purposes, and a taxpayer may not deduct such space as an office.

However, there has been a liberalization of this rule in some parts of the country where the courts have held that a studio or an office can exist in a room that has a personal use, so long as a clearly defined area is used exclusively for business. It is important to remember that, generally, the IRS functions on a regional basis. Except for issues that have been reserved for decision by the National Office, each IRS office is independent and makes its own decisions until the United States Supreme Court or Congress makes a decision that applies nationally. That is why the decision by a circuit court in one area may not apply elsewhere.

The requirement regarding regular use means that the use of the room may not be merely incidental or occasional. Obviously, there is a gray area between regular and occasional. Perhaps some business owners just starting up can use this rule as an inducement to overcome temporary bouts of laziness or ennui. If you are planning on deducting any expenses for your home office, you must keep working to satisfy the regularity test.

Like the regularity requirement, the rule regarding the principal place of business has been very vague. However, under a proposed IRS regulation, a taxpayer may have a different principal place of business for each trade or business in which that person is engaged. The test requires looking at the particular facts of each case but, generally, the key elements are these: (1) the amount of income derived from the business done there; (2) the amount of time spent there; and (3) the nature of the facility.

Thus it is now possible, for example, for a dentist whose principal place of business (judging by income and time spent) is at a clinic to also run a sideline business of selling cosmetics out of the home and to claim the home office as the principal place of business for the cosmetics enterprise.

In *Meiers v. Commissioner* the plaintiff owned a self-service laundromat. Mrs. Meiers managed the business, supervised the five part-time employees, and performed other managerial and bookkeeping functions. She spent only about an hour a day at the laundromat and two hours a day in her office at home. The office was used exclusively for activities related to business. The tax court ruled that since the laundromat was the "focal point" of the business, any deduction for an office in the home should be disallowed.

The Court of Appeals for the Seventh Circuit reversed that decision, holding that, rather than using the focal point of the business as the basis of its decision, the tax court should have looked to the principal place of the taxpayer's activities. Managerial decisions were made from the office, and a conscious decision was made not to create an office at the laundromat itself. For these reasons, the office-at-home deduction was allowed.

In another case, the tax court disallowed a claim for an office-at-home deduction despite a unique argument. In *Baie v. Commissioner*, the taxpayers operated a hot dog stand some distance from their home. Because the stand measured only 10 feet by 10 feet, some of the food preparation and storage was done at home. The ruling by the tax court was based on the fact that the kitchen and storage areas were not used exclusively for business purposes.

The taxpayers used the argument that they were actually engaged in a manufacturing operation at home; therefore, the office-at-home section of the IRC did not apply. The court held that the statute included such an operation, and the deduction was not allowed.

Another tax court decision denying the office-at-home deduction was *Moller v. United States*. The taxpayers were a husband and wife who claimed a deduction for the area of their home used to manage their investments. The court held that in order to qualify as a trade or business, the business must consist of the active buying and selling of securities, with income derived therefrom. The Mollers, however, derived their income from the dividends and interest resulting from holding securities for a long time. This, the court held, did not rise to the level of carrying on a trade or business.

When the office is in a structure separate from the principal residence, the requirements for deductibility are less stringent. The structure must be used exclusively and on a regular basis, just as an office in the home itself; however, when the office is in a separate structure, it need only be used "in connection with" the business, not as the principal place of business.

When taxpayers use a portion of their homes for storage of business materials (as well as for business), the requirements for deductibility of the storage area are also less stringent. The dwelling must be the sole fixed location of the business, and the storage area must be used on a regular basis for the storage of the business equipment or products. The room used for storage need not be used entirely or exclusively for business, but there must be a "separately identifiable space suitable for storage" of the business-related materials.

Is the Office-at-Home Deduction Worthwhile? If a taxpayer meets one of the tests outlined above, the next question is what tax benefits can result. The answer, after close analysis, is frequently "not very many." An allocable portion of mortgage interest and property taxes can be deducted against the business. These would be deductible anyway as itemized deductions. The advantage of deducting them against the business is that this reduces the business profit that is subject to self-employment taxes.

Of course, a taxpayer who lives in a rented house and otherwise qualifies for the office-at-home deductions may deduct a portion of the rent that would not otherwise be tax-deductible.

The primary tax advantage comes from a deduction for an allocable portion of repairs, utility bills, and depreciation. Otherwise, these would not be deductible at all.

To arrive at the allocable portion, take the square footage of the space used for the business and divide that by the total square footage of the house. Multiply this fraction by your mortgage interest, property taxes, and so forth, for the amount to be deducted. How to determine the amount of allowable depreciation is too complex to discuss here, and you should discuss this with your accountant or tax adviser.

The total amount that can be deducted for an office or storage place in the home is artificially limited. To determine the amount that can be deducted, take the total amount of money earned in the business and subtract the allocable portion of mortgage interest and property taxes, and other deductions allocable to the business. The remainder is the maximum amount that you can deduct for the allocable portion of repairs, utilities, and depreciation. In other words, your total business deductions in this situation cannot be greater than your total business income minus all other business expenses. The office-at-home deduction, therefore, cannot be used to create a net loss. Disallowed losses can, however, be carried forward indefinitely and deducted in future years against profits from the business.

Besides the obvious complexity of the rules and the mathematics, there are several other factors that limit the benefit of taking a deduction for a studio or office in the home. One of these is the partial loss of the nonrecognition of gain (tax-deferred) treatment that is otherwise allowed when a taxpayer sells a personal residence. Ordinarily, when someone sells a personal residence for profit, the tax on the gain is deferred if the seller purchases another personal residence of at least the same value within two years. Most of the tax on this gain is never paid during the taxpayer's lifetime.

This deferral of gain, however, is not allowed to the extent that the house was used in the business. This means that the taxpayer must pay tax on the allocable portion of the gain from the sale.

For example, if you have been claiming 20 percent of your home as a business deduction, when you sell the home you will enjoy a tax deferral on only 80 percent of the profit. The other 20 percent will be subject to tax because that 20 percent represents the sale of a business asset.

In essence, for the price of a current deduction you may be converting what is essentially a nonrecognition, or tax-deferred, asset into a trade or business property.

However, there is one important exception that can work to your advantage. The IRS has ruled that if you stop qualifying for the office-at-home tax deduction for at least one year before you sell the house, you are entitled to the entire gain as a rollover, no matter how many years you have been taking the deduction. (A rollover means you can reinvest the proceeds of the sale in another dwelling within the prescribed period and avoid paying taxes.)

The word "qualifying" in the IRS ruling has a very important meaning. It does not mean only that you stop taking the business deduction for one year. It means that you physically move the business out of your home so that it no longer qualifies as an office at home, whether or not you take it as a tax deduction. The same ruling applies to the one-time tax exemption of up to $125,000 on the sale of a home by persons over age 55. If you plan to sell your home any time soon, check all this out with an accountant or tax adviser. A little planning might save you a great deal of money.

Another concern is that by deducting for an office in the home, the taxpayer in effect puts a red flag on the tax return. Obviously, when the tax return expressly asks whether expenses are being deducted for an office in the home, the question is not being asked for purely academic reasons. Although only the IRS knows how much the answer to this question affects someone's chances of being audited, there is no doubt that a "yes" answer does increase the likelihood of an audit.

Given this increased possibility of audit, it generally does not pay to deduct for home office expenses in doubtful situations. Taxpayers who lose the deduction must pay back taxes plus interest or fight in court. One unfortunate taxpayer not only lost the deduction on a technicality but also lost the rollover treatment on the sale of his home.

If you believe that your office at home could qualify for the business deduction, you would be well advised to consult with a competent tax expert who can assist in calculating the deduction.

2. *Other Deductions*

Charitable Deductions   The law provides that an individual or business can donate either money or property to qualified charities and take a tax deduction for the donation. Individuals are afforded more favorable deductions for donations of money or property they own than are artists donating their own creations or businesspeople who donate property out of their inventory. Since this area can be quite technical, you should consult with your tax adviser before making any charitable donations. In addition, there have been some abuses on the part of charities that resulted in misappropriation of donated funds. If you have any question about the validity of a particular charity, you should contact your state Attorney General's Office or the local governmental agency that polices charitable solicitations in your area.

Grants, Prizes, and Awards   Individuals who receive income from grants or fellowships should be aware that this income can be excluded from gross income and thus represents considerable tax savings. To qualify for this exclusion, the grant must be for the purpose of furthering one's education and training. However, amounts received under a grant or fellowship that are specifically designated to cover expenses related to the grant are no longer fully deductible. Furthermore, if the grant is given as compensation for services or is primarily for the benefit of the grant-giving organization, it cannot be excluded.

For scholarships and fellowships granted after August 16, 1986, the deduction is allowed only if the recipient is a degree candidate. The amount of the exclusion from income is limited to the amounts used for tuition, fees, books, supplies, and equipment. Amounts designated for room, board, and other incidental expenses are included in income. No exclusion from income is allowed for recipients who are not degree candidates.

The above rules apply to income from grants and fellowships. Unfortunately, the Tax Reform Act of 1986 also put tighter restrictions on money, goods, or services received as prizes or awards. Previously, the amounts received for certain awards were excluded from income if the recipient was rewarded for past achievements and had not applied for the award. Examples of this type of award are the Pulitzer Prize or the Nobel Prize. Under the present law, any prizes or awards for religious, charitable, scientific, or artistic achievements are included as income to the recipient unless the prize is assigned to charity.

If you do not know whether a particular activity is deductible, you should consult with a competent CPA or tax adviser before embarking on it.

3. *Capital Gains Tax.* Until just recently, the capital gains tax was nothing more than a relic of the past. The capital gains preference has been and still is a hot topic for partisan debate. In 1991, a modest capital gains preference was reinstated, setting a 28 percent tax cap on assets disposed of that produce a capital gain. For persons in the middle-to-low income tax bracket, the capital gains tax is meaningless. But for individuals in the top (31 percent) tax bracket, it means a 3 percent tax reduction on the income realized any time an asset that produces a capital gain is disposed of.

The key to a working understanding of the capital gains tax is the definition of a ''capital asset.'' Capital assets are items of property held by the taxpayer, often for investment purposes. The law does not clearly define a capital asset, but it does identify items that are *not* capital assets. Among other things, capital asset does not include property used in a trade or business that is subject to the rules for depreciation, inventory held for sale, or real property used in the trade or business. All other property held by the taxpayer is a capital asset—

for example, the stock held in the incorporated practice (or any other business in which the taxpayer holds stock).

When a capital asset is sold, the net amount realized, minus the adjusted "basis" of the asset (the acquisition price minus such things as the amount of any depreciation taken against it) and selling expense, is a capital gain or loss. Capital gains or losses also result from the sale of other property besides capital assets. These exceptions will be discussed below.

Other Property Subject to Capital Gain or Loss Rules   The sale or exchange of property other than capital assets can result in a capital gain or loss. Basically, any property that can have basis can produce capital gain or loss on disposition in the right set of circumstances.

The sale of inventory does not result in a capital gain or loss even if the inventory is sold in bulk. There may be a different result if the entire practice is sold and then liquidated but, if the inventory is sold at an advertised liquidation, the taxpayer has a good argument that the inventory was sold as goods to customers, resulting in ordinary gain or loss.

Except for like-kind exchanges, the sale of real estate owned and used by a business, including long-term leaseholds, or the sale of depreciable business property such as furniture or equipment, can result in capital gain.

These are called "section 1231" gains and losses. If all the sales of section 1231 property result in a net section 1231 gain for the year, the net gain is treated as capital gain. But if section 1231 losses for the year exceed section 1231 gains, the resulting net loss is treated as ordinary loss and may be used to offset ordinary income without limit. The rule is fairly simple for the first year in which section 1231 loss occurs. However, the taxpayer must keep track of his section 1231 losses, for the next five years following their occurrence. Each time the taxpayer uses a net 1231 loss to offset ordinary income, the amount must be dated and posted to a hypothetical "recapture account." Any section 1231 net gain occurring over the next five years must be reported as ordinary income to the extent of the amount in the recapture account. The idea is that the tax benefit gained by treating capital losses as ordinary will be erased over time by treating capital gains as ordinary income.

Thankfully, section 1231 does not apply to property held for one year or less. Sale of short-term property of this type yields ordinary income or ordinary loss.

The technicality of the capital gains tax serves to illustrate the immense complexity of the IRC. The Code is full of pitfalls for the unwary; however, with the aid of a competent tax adviser, one can avoid these pitfalls and hopefully reduce the pinch of any taxing situation.

15

Pension Plans

This chapter will provide a general understanding of the nature of qualified pension plans and how to select the most appropriate plan.

Before delving into plan designs and investments, it is important to understand what a qualified plan is, what it will accomplish, and how it will accomplish what it is intended to do for the medical professional.

In simplest terms, a qualified plan is a savings program memorialized in writing, which meets specific applicable rules and regulations of the IRS. If the plan meets the IRS's design criteria, contributions are tax-deductible to the person or business making the investments. The earnings of these investments will grow free of all taxes either to the plan sponsor or the participants.

A qualified plan is the last remaining tax shelter available to highly compensated individuals. It may be used to set aside funds for the professional's retirement, and to attract and retain key employees. If properly structured and funded on a conservative basis with diversified portfolio investments, the professional should achieve financial security for retirement. It should be noted that this may be an extremely elusive goal in that, statistically, fewer than 1 in 17 physicians actually achieve full financial independence for their retirement.

To facilitate your understanding of qualified plans and their investments, this chapter has been divided into two areas. The first portion will discuss concepts and plan design. The second portion will deal with the types of investments that can be made through a qualified plan. In adopting a qualified plan, care should be taken to select the type of plan that will most satisfactorily meet your needs. Choosing the plan most appropriate for you is based on a series of factors.

Types of Plans

There are three categories of qualified plans: Defined Contribution, Defined Benefit, and Target Benefit.

Defined Contribution Plans

There are several types of defined contribution plans. Defined contribution plans are all identical, in that the *contributions* to the plan are defined. The amount of money that is invested on behalf of the participant is defined as a percentage of the annual income of the participant. The amount of money that will be available to the participant at retirement is *NOT DEFINED*. Plans of this type include profit-sharing plans, money purchase plans, and salary savings or reduction plans (such as 401K).

Profit-Sharing Plans   If the revenue (income) from your practice varies significantly from year to year, a profit-sharing plan may be most appropriate. Contributions to a profit-sharing plan are determined at the end of the accounting year of the practice, usually December 31. These contributions to the plan *must be* made by the due date of the tax return including any extensions. Contributions to the plan can be determined annually by a vote of your business's governing board (i.e., Board of Directors of a professional corporation, or managing partner), or by a formula previously designated in the plan's documents. Recent changes in federal laws no longer necessitate a corporation having to declare a profit in order to make a contribution.

Contributions to a profit-sharing plan are limited to a maximum of 15 percent of an employee's annual income and cannot exceed total contributions of $30,000 per year for each participant.

Salary Reduction/Savings Plans Such As 401K, Also Known as Thrift Plans   These plans are a variant of profit-sharing plans. Under this type of plan, the employee elects to have a percentage of his or her gross salary diverted into the qualified plan. Depending on the plan, the *employer* may elect to match a portion of the contributions made by the *employee*. Usually this matching of contributions has a limit. Contributions made by the employee are pretax dollars; therefore, a significant tax savings can be accomplished for the employee through utilization of the plan.

The main emphasis of salary reduction plans has been to shift a portion of the funding from the employer over to the employee. By shifting some of the cost to the employee/participant, the business is able to reduce its cash contribution to the plan.

A major drawback to the use of this type of program is the limitation of contributions by highly compensated employees. In addition to a maximum limitation, for 1991, of approximately $8475, total contributions to the plan on behalf of the top one-third highly compensated employees are dictated by those on behalf of the lower two-thirds compensated employees. Although there are exceptions, generally this plan should be utilized only in instances where the company has at least 25 employees.

Simplified Employee Pension Plans (SEPs)   These plans are incorrectly viewed by many as an alternative to the more highly structured qualified plans. However, their simplicity results in a significant inflexibility that most professionals are not willing to accept. Furthermore, these plans operate under those statutes that pertain to IRAs. For example, the contributions made under these plans on behalf of plan participants are paid into segregated accounts, held on behalf of the participant. These are IRA accounts and accordingly *do not* enjoy the immunity from civil claims (professional liability) and bankruptcy that assets held in self-employed and corporate qualified plans have. Generally, the limitations are a maximum contribution of $30,000 per annum with contributions based on an equal percentage of annual salary for *all* employees 21 years or older who have performed service for the employer during at least three out of five years, and who have received at least $363.00. It is basically an employer-funded IRA. Although its low maintenance cost is an initial attraction for its use, its relative inflexibility has minimized its use by many employers.

Money Purchase Plan Under this type of plan, the professional determines how much he or she wants to save each year. Although there are other restrictions, the primary parameters are: the lesser of 25 percent of annual income (20 percent for a self-employed individual), not to exceed $30,000 in contributions per year per participant.

In each of the above plans, contributions on behalf of each participant are determined solely on the basis of annual income. Interest and earnings on the investments made through the plan are used to increase the retirement benefit for the individual participants. A significant factor is the time over which the investments are made. The longer the period of time over which investments are accumulated and the interest is earned, the greater the amount of benefits that will be available to the participant at retirement.

Employee Stock Ownership Plans (ESOPs) An Employee Stock Ownership Plan is another type of defined contribution plan. In a normal defined contribution plan, the trustee is specifically prohibited from retaining (owning) more than 10 percent of the stock in the parent corporation. An ESOP is the exception. Under this type of program, the majority of the plan's assets are, in fact, shares of stock in the parent corporation. Generally, ESOPs are not useful for professional corporations since most states require shareholders of professional corporations to be licensed in the profession practiced by the PC. (See the discussion on PCs in Chapter 2.)

Defined Benefit Plans

Contributions to a Defined Benefit Plan are determined by a relatively complex formula that is then monitored by an Enrolled Actuary. An Enrolled Actuary is an individual professionally licensed to review or evaluate qualified plans. Generally, this type of plan is used to favor the more senior employee/participant with fewer than 10 working years before retirement age. In the proper situation, this plan can "draw out" significant amounts of money from the professional's practice on a very favorable tax basis.

Contributions to a defined benefit plan are limited to the amount of contributions necessary to fund a *retirement benefit* for each participant not to exceed the lesser of 100 percent of their annual average income for their three high consecutive years or $108,963 per year as of January 1, 1991. The figures will change annually based on inflation.

Excess earnings (investment income) greater than the actuarial assumption (normally 8 percent) are used to reduce the cost of the plan for the professional.

Normally, defined benefit plans are appropriate where the professional is "mature," with less than 10 working years until retirement (normally 66), and the practice has enjoyed considerable financial success. Under these circumstances, the defined benefit plan can be designed to drain excess funds and allocate them to retirement. In many instances, this same advantage can be attained through the use of a target benefit plan.

Target Benefit Plans

A third category of plan that is receiving renewed interest, as a result of changes in income tax law, is the target benefit plan. This plan is actually a hybrid plan *combining* the recognition for senior (older) employees found in defined benefit plans, with the contribution levels and benefit levels of a defined contribution plan. As a result of changes under the Technical Corrections Act of 1987, a second addition to this hybrid category, known as an age-weighted profit-sharing plan, has been developed. As with the target benefit plan, the contributions to this profit-sharing plan are weighted, or skewed, toward senior employees.

Since 1982, federal tax laws were amended to allow unincorporated businesses the same status as corporate qualified plans. Furthermore, this same legislation eliminated the need for a third-party administrator, thus allowing the employer to be the trustee (caretaker, responsible party) of his or her own plan.

Plans may be combined or "stacked" to more specifically meet the needs of the business. However, this stacking creates separate sets of rules and limitations. Additionally, it increases the amount of administrative paperwork and forms, thus driving up the cost of operating and maintaining the plan.

Design Considerations

Plan Documentation

As previously noted, the plan must be in writing. The creation of a qualified plan usually involves the creation and adoption of a trust agreement, disclosure of information for employees, and other pertinent language. Plans containing the standardized language that has been preapproved by the IRS are routinely available from several sources, including insurance companies, brokerage houses, and mutual fund companies. Each of these sources may have limitations, either in the language, investment opportunities, or requirements for the use of a third-party trustee, that should be carefully evaluated. It is, therefore, essential to work with an experienced professional when selecting and establishing a plan.

The design features outlined below are used either to limit or reduce the cost or participation by employees in the employer-sponsored plan.

Vesting

A key element of any qualified plan is to reward long-term service by employees. One method used to limit the participation by employees who are employed for a relatively short period of time is through the use of a vesting schedule. Currently, for small plans, the IRS recognizes two primary vesting formulas. These are:

1. Five-year exclusion with 100 percent vesting. Also known as "cliff" vesting, since it is like falling off a cliff, that is, all or nothing. This formula does not allow vesting for employees with less than five years of service. Upon the completion of five years' service, the employee is immediately 100 percent vested in the plan.

2. Three- to seven-year graded vesting. This vesting formula can preclude participation by an employee for at least 12 months following the date of employment until the employee has worked for at least one plan year. Following completion of the third plan year of employment, for the subsequent 12 months the employee would be entitled to 20 percent of the funds that have been set aside for him or her. For each subsequent year of participation in the plan, the employee is vested an additional 20 percent. Fol-

lowing the completion of seven years of plan participation, the employee would be eligible to receive 100 percent of the contributions and interest earnings on the funds, upon termination of employment.

Minimum Hours

The plan sponsor may limit the participation of employees by exempting from participation employees who work less than 500 hours per year. This feature is very important for the professional who retains temporary employees.

Minimum Age

Another manner by which the plan sponsor can limit participation of employees is through the use of a minimum age requirement. Current law allows an employer to postpone participation by employees under 21 years of age. It should be noted that at the time the employee reaches age 21, his or her total years of service must be applied to the vesting formula.

Integration

This feature allows the plan sponsor to recognize contributions made on behalf of the employee to Social Security. Under this feature, the plan sponsor applies two separate levels of contribution. The first level is a minimum contribution up to the maximum contributions under Social Security. Current tax statutes limit the separation of the two levels of contributions to 7 percent.

Union

A final manner in which the plan sponsor can exempt the participation of certain employee groups is through their participation in a union. Employees that are a part of a collective bargaining unit can be specifically exempted from participation in a qualified plan established by an employer.

Investments in a Qualified Plan

The primary governing factor regarding investments by a qualified plan is contained in the IRC statement known generally as "The Prudent Person Investment Principle." This means that investments made by a qualified plan should be made with paramount consideration to preservation of principal (amounts invested) or salary with growth and income as secondary considerations.

Growth

In an investment, growth occurs where the original principal or amount invested increases in value; for example, the purchase of shares of stock at $1.00 per share that increase in value to $1.25 per share.

Income

Income or interest is derived through a principal investment earning interest. An example of this would be bonds or a money market account. As a result of the plethora of investment opportunities, two of the most frequent questions asked are: "What investments should I use in my pension plan?" and "How much should I invest in each one?"

Since the opportunities are virtually infinite, including stocks, bonds, real estate, partnership interests, and the like, it is essential for you to confer with an experienced qualified financial planner who should be able to assist with structuring your plan investments based on your goals, the economy, and other relevant factors.

16

Estate Planning

Proper estate planning will require the assistance of a knowledgeable lawyer and perhaps also a life insurance agent, an accountant, or a bank trust officer, depending on the nature and size of the estate. In this chapter we will consider the basic principles of estate planning. This discussion is not a substitute for the aid of a lawyer experienced in estate planning; rather, it is intended to introduce you to the basic principles, alert you to potential problems, and aid in preparing you to work with your estate planner(s). It should be noted that the law of wills and disposition of property varies from state to state. In addition, some states have unique rules for couples known as community property laws. It is, therefore, important to deal with an attorney who is familiar with the relevant state laws.

The Will

A will is a legal instrument by which a person directs the distribution of property in his or her estate upon death. The maker of the will is called the *testator*. Gifts given by a will are referred to as *bequests* (personal property) or *devises* (real estate). Certain formalities are required by state law to create a valid will. About thirty states allow *only* formally witnessed wills; they require that the instrument be in writing and signed by the testator, in the presence of two or more witnesses. The other half of the states allow *either* witnessed or unwitnessed wills. If a will is entirely handwritten and signed by the testator, it is known as a holographic will.

A will is a unique document in two respects. First, if properly drafted it is *ambulatory*, meaning it can accommodate change, such as applying to property acquired after the will is made. Second, a will is *revocable*, meaning that the testator has the power to change or cancel it. Even if a testator makes a valid agreement not to revoke the will, the power to revoke it remains, though liability for breach of contract could result.

Generally, courts do not consider a will to have been revoked unless it can be established that the testator either (1) performed a physical act of revocation, such as burning or tearing up a will, with intent to revoke it; or (2) executed a valid later will that revoked the previous will. Most state statutes also provide for automatic revocation of a will in whole or in part if the testator is subsequently divorced or married.

To modify a will, the testator must execute a supplement, known as a codicil, which has the same formal requirements as those for creating a will. To the extent that the codicil contradicts the will, those contradicted parts of the will are revoked.

Payment of Testator's Debts

When the property owned by the testator at death is insufficient to satisfy all the bequests in the will after all debts and taxes have been paid, some or all of the bequests in the will must be reduced or even eliminated entirely. The process of reducing or eliminating bequests is known as *abatement*, and the priorities for reduction are set according to the category of each bequest. The legally significant categories of gifts are generally as follows: *specific* bequests or devises, meaning gifts of identifiable items ("I give to X all the furniture in my home"); *demonstrative* bequests or devises, meaning gifts that are to be paid out of a specified source unless that source contains insufficient funds, in which case the gifts will be paid out of the general assets ("I give to Y $1000 to be paid from my shares of stock in ABC Corporation"); *general* bequests, meaning gifts payable out of the general assets of an estate ("I give Z $1000"); and finally, *residuary* bequests or devises, or gifts of whatever is left in the estate after all other gifts and expenses are satisfied ("I give the rest, residue, and remainder of my estate to Z").

Intestate property, or property not governed by a will, is usually the first to be taken to satisfy claims against the state. (If the will contains a valid residuary clause, there will be no such property.) Next, residuary bequests will be taken. If more money is needed, general bequests will be taken, and lastly, specific and demonstrative bequests will be taken together in proportion to their value. Some states provide that all gifts, regardless of type, abate proportionately.

Disposition of Property Not Willed

If the testator acquires more property during the time between signing the will and death, the disposition of such property will also be governed by the will, which, as we have seen, is ambulatory in nature. If such property falls within the description of an existing category in the will ("I give all my stock to X; I give all my real estate to Y"), it will pass along with all similar property. If it does not, and the will contains a valid residuary clause, such after-acquired property will go to the residuary legatees. If there is no such clause that applies to this property, such property will pass outside the will to the persons specified in the state's law of intestate succession.

When a person dies without leaving a valid will, this is known as dying *intestate*. The property of a person who dies intestate is distributed according to the state law of intestate succession, which specifies who is entitled to what parts of the estate. An intestate's surviving spouse will always receive a share, generally at least one-third of the estate. An intestate's surviving children likewise always get a share. If some of the children do not survive the intestate, the grandchildren of the intestate may be entitled to a share by representation. *Representation* is a legal principle that means if an heir does not survive the decedent but has a child who does survive, that child will represent the nonsurviving heir and receive that parent's share in the estate. In other words, the surviving child stands in the shoes of a dead parent in order to inherit from a grandparent who dies intestate.

If there are no direct descendants surviving, the intestate's surviving spouse will take the entire estate or share it with the intestate's parents. If there is neither a surviving spouse nor any surviving direct descendant of the intestate, the estate will be distributed to the intestate's parents or, if the parents are not surviving, to the intestate's siblings by representation. If there are no surviving persons in any of these categories, the estate will go to surviving grandparents and their direct descendants. In this way, the family tree is constantly expanded in search of surviving relatives. If none of the persons specified in the law of intestate succession survive the testator, the intestate's property ultimately goes to the state. This is known as *escheat*. It should be noted that the laws of intestate succession make no provision for friends, in-laws, or stepchildren.

State law will often provide a testator's surviving spouse with certain benefits from the estate even if the spouse is left out of the testator's will. Historically, these benefits were known as *dower*, in the case of a surviving wife, or *curtesy*, in the case of a surviving husband. In place of the old dower and curtesy, modern statutes give the surviving spouse the right to "elect" against the will, and thereby receive a share equal to at least one-fourth of the estate. Here again, state laws vary; in some states, the surviving spouse's elective share is one-third. The historical concepts of dower and curtesy are in large part a result of the law's traditional recognition of an absolute duty on the part of the husband to provide for the wife. Modern laws are perhaps better justified by the notion that most property in a marriage should be shared, because the financial success of either partner is due to the efforts of both.

Advantages to Having a Will

Now that we have some background as to what a will is and what happens without one, we can begin to look at some of the benefits of having a will.

A will affords the opportunity to direct distribution of one's property and to set out limitations by making gifts conditional. For example, if an individual wishes to donate certain property to a specific charity but only if certain conditions are adhered to, a will can make such conditions a prerequisite to the donation.

A will permits the testator to nominate an executor, called a "personal representative" in some states, to administer the estate. If no executor is named in the will, the court will appoint one. If the testator has an unusual type of property, such as antiques, art, or publishable manuscripts, it is a good idea to appoint joint executors, one with financial expertise and the other with expertise in valuation of antiques, or in art, or with publishing. If joint executors are used, some provision should be made in the will for resolving any deadlock between the two. For example, a neutral third party might be appointed as an arbitrator who is directed to resolve any impasses after hearing both sides. It is also advisable to define the scope of the executor's power by detailed instructions. A lawyer's help will be necessary to set forth all of these important considerations in legally enforceable, unambiguous terms. It is essential in a will to avoid careless language that might be subject to attack by survivors unhappy with the will's provisions. A lawyer's help is also crucial to avoid making bequests that are not legally enforceable because contrary to public policy.

In addition to giving the testator significant posthumous control over division of property, a carefully drafted will can greatly reduce the overall amount of estate tax paid at death. The following information on taxing structures relates to federal estate taxation. State estate taxes often contain similar provisions, but state law must always be consulted for specifics.

The Gross Estate

The first step in evaluating an estate for tax purposes is to determine the so-called "gross estate." The *gross estate* will include all property over which the deceased had significant control at the time of death. Examples would include certain life insurance proceeds and annuities, jointly held interests, stock in a professional corporation, and revocable transfers.

Under current tax laws, the executor of an estate may elect to value the property in the estate either as of the date of death or as of a date six months after death. The estate property must be valued in its entirety at the time chosen. However, if the executor elects to value the estate six months after death and certain pieces of property are distributed or sold before then, that property will be valued as of the date of distribution or sale.

Fair market value is defined as the price at which property would change hands between a willing buyer and a willing seller, when both buyer and seller have reasonable knowledge of all relevant facts. Such a determination is often very difficult to make, especially when items such as artwork are involved. Although the initial determination of fair market value is generally made by the executor when the estate tax return is filed, the IRS may disagree with the executor's valuation and assign assets a much higher fair market value.

When an executor and the IRS disagree as to valuation, the court will decide the matter. In most cases, the burden will be on the taxpayer to prove the value of the asset. Thus, expert testimony and evidence of the sale of the same or similar properties will be helpful, as in cases involving original manuscripts and drawings. In general, courts are reluctant to determine valuation by formula.

Generally, estate taxes must be paid when the estate tax return is filed (within nine months of the date of death) although arrangements may be made to spread payments out over a number of years, if necessary. It is not uncommon for executors to be forced to sell properties for less than full value in order to pay taxes. This can be avoided by obtaining insurance policies, the proceeds of which can be set up in a trust. (For an explanation of a trust, see the section "Distributing Property Outside the Will" below.)

The law allows a number of deductions from the gross estate in determining the amount of the taxable estate. The taxable estate is the basis upon which the tax owed is computed. The following section gives you a closer look at some of the key deductions used to arrive at the amount of your taxable estate.

The Taxable Estate

Figuring the taxable estate is the second major step in evaluating an estate for tax purposes after determining the gross estate. Typical deductions from the gross estate include funeral expenses; certain estate administration expenses; debts and enforceable claims against the estate; mortgages and liens; and, perhaps most significant, the marital deduction and the charitable deduction.

The marital deduction allows the total value of any interest in property that passes from the decedent to the surviving spouse to be subtracted from the value of the gross estate. The government will eventually get its tax on this property when the spouse dies, but only to the extent such interest is included in the spouse's gross estate. This deduction may occur even in the absence of a will making a gift to the surviving spouse, since state law generally provides that the spouse is entitled to at least one-fourth of the overall estate regardless of the provisions of the will.

The charitable deduction refers to the tax deduction allowed upon the transfer of property from an estate to a recognized charity. Since the definition of a charity for tax purposes is quite technical, it is advisable to insert a clause in the will that provides that if the institution specified to receive the donation does not qualify for the charitable deduction, the bequest shall go to a substitute qualified institution at the choice of the executor.

Once deductions are figured, the taxable estate is taxed at the rate specified by the Unified Estate and Gift Tax Schedule. The unified tax imposes the same rate of tax on gifts made by will as on gifts made during life. It is a progressive tax, meaning the percent paid in taxes increases with the amount of property involved. The rates rise significantly for larger estates, for example, from 18 percent where the cumulative total of taxable estate and taxable gifts is under $10,000 to 55 percent where the cumulative total is over $3,000,000. Tax credits are provided by year according to the tax schedule. Federal estate tax is also reduced by state death tax credit or actual state death tax, whichever is less. Tax credits result in a $600,000 exemption, which is available to every estate. This exemption, combined with the unlimited marital deduction, allows most estates to escape estate taxes altogether.

Distributing Property Outside the Will

Property can be distributed outside of the will by making *inter vivos* gifts (given during the giver's lifetime) either outright or by placing the property in trust prior to death. The main advantage to distributing property outside of the will is that the property escapes the delays and expense of probate, the court procedure by which a will is validated and administered. It used to be that there were also significant tax advantages to making *inter vivos* gifts rather than gifts by will, but since the estate and gift-tax rates are now unified, there are few remaining tax advantages. One remaining advantage to making an *inter vivos* gift is that if the gift appreciates in value between the time the gift is made and death, the appreciated value will not be taxed. If the gift were made by will, the added value would be taxable since the gift would be valued as of date of death (or six months after). This value difference can represent significant tax savings for the heirs of someone whose practice suddenly becomes successful and rapidly increases in value.

The other advantage to making an *inter vivos* gift involves the yearly exclusion. A yearly exclusion of $10,000 per recipient is available on *inter vivos* gifts. For example, if $15,000 worth of gifts were given to an individual in one year, only $5,000 worth of gifts will actually be taxable to the donor (who is responsible for the gift tax). A married couple can combine their gifts and claim a yearly exclusion of $20,000 per recipient. Gifts made within three years of death used to be included in the gross estate on the theory that they were made in contemplation of death. Recent amendments to the tax laws, however, have done away with the three-year rule for most purposes. The three-year rule is still applicable to gifts of life insurance and to certain transfers involving stock redemptions or tax liens; the rule also applies to certain valuation schemes, the details of which are too complex to discuss here.

Gift-tax returns must be filed by the donor for any year where gifts made exceeded $10,000 to any one donee. It is not necessary to file returns when a gift to any one donee amounts to less than $10,000. However, where it is possible that valuation of the gift will become an issue with the IRS, it may be a good idea to file a return anyway. Filing the return starts the three-year statute of limitations running. Once the statute of limitations period has expired, the IRS will be barred from filing suit for unpaid taxes or for tax deficiencies due to higher government valuations of the gifts. If a taxpayer omits includable gifts amounting to more than 25 percent of the total amount of gifts stated in the return, the statute of limitations is extended to six years. There is no statute of limitations for fraudulent returns filed with the intent to evade tax.

In order to qualify as an *inter vivos* (living) gift for tax purposes, a gift must be complete and final. Control is an important issue. If a giver retains the right to revoke a gift, the gift may be found testamentary in nature, even if the right to revoke was never exercised (unless the gift was made in trust). The gift must also be delivered. An actual, physical delivery is best, but a symbolic delivery may suffice if there is strong evidence of intent to make an irrevocable gift. An example of symbolic delivery is when the donor puts something in a safe and gives the intended recipient the only key.

Another common way to transfer property outside the will is to place the property in a trust that is created prior to death. A *trust* is simply a legal arrangement by which one person holds certain property for the benefit of another. The person holding the property is the *trustee*; those for whose benefit it is held are the *beneficiaries*. To create a valid trust, the giver must identify the trust property; make a declaration of intent to create the trust; transfer property to the trust; and name identifiable beneficiaries. If no trustee is named, a court will appoint one. The settlor, or creator of the trust, may also be designated as trustee, in which case segregation of the trust property satisfies the delivery requirement. Trusts can be created by will, in which case they are termed testamentary trusts, but these trust properties will be probated along with the rest of the will. To avoid probate, the settlor must create a valid *inter vivos* trust—one given while the giver is alive.

Generally, in order to qualify as an *inter vivos* trust, a valid interest in property must be transferred before the death of the creator of the trust. If the settlor fails to name a beneficiary for the trust or make delivery of the property to the trustee before death, the trust will likely be termed testamentary. Such a trust will be deemed invalid unless the formalities required for creating a will were complied with.

A trust will not be termed testamentary simply because the settlor retained significant control over the trust, such as the power to revoke or modify the trust. For example, when a person makes a deposit in a savings account in his or her own name as trustee for another, and reserves the power to withdraw the money or revoke the trust, the trust will be enforceable by the beneficiary upon the death of the depositor, providing the depositor has not in fact revoked the trust. Many states allow the same type of arrangement in authorizing joint bank accounts with rights of survivorship as valid will substitutes. Property transferred under one of these arrangements is thus passed outside the will and need not go through probate. However, even though such an arrangement escapes probate, the trust property will probably be counted as part of the gross estate for tax purposes because the settlor retained significant control. In addition, if the deceased settlor created a revocable trust for the purpose of decreasing the share of a surviving spouse, in some states the trust will be declared illusory—in effect, invalid. The surviving spouse is then granted the legal share not only from the probated estate but from the revocable trust.

Life insurance trusts can be used for paying estate taxes. The proceeds will not be taxed if the life insurance trust is irrevocable and the beneficiary is someone other than the estate, such as a friend or relative in an individual capacity or the practice. This is especially important for medical professionals, since without a life insurance trust their survivors might be forced to sell estate assets for less than their real value in order to pay estate taxes.

All medical professionals should give some thought to estate planning and take the time to execute a will. Without a will, there is simply no way to control the disposition of one's property. Sound estate planning may include transfers outside of the will, since these types of arrangements escape the delays and expenses of probate. Certain types of trusts can be valuable will substitutes, but they may be subject to challenge by a surviving spouse. Since successful estate planning is complex, it is essential to work with a lawyer skilled in this field.

17

How to Find a Lawyer
or an Accountant

M ost medical practitioners expect to seek the advice of a lawyer only occasionally, for counseling on important matters such as the decision to incorporate or the purchase of a building. If this is your concept of the attorney's role in your practice, I recommend that you reevaluate it. Most health care professionals would operate more efficiently and more profitably in the long run if they had a relationship with a business attorney more like that between a doctor and patient— that is, an ongoing relationship that allows the attorney to get to know the business well enough to engage in preventive legal counseling and assist in planning, thus making possible the solution of many problems before they occur.

If your practice is small now or undercapitalized, you are doubtless anxious to keep operating costs down. You probably do not relish the idea of paying an attorney to get to know your practice if you are not involved in an immediate crisis. However, it is a good bet that a visit with a competent business lawyer right now will result in the raising of issues vital to the future of your practice. There is good reason why larger, successful practices employ one or more attorneys full time as in-house counsel. Ready access to legal advice is something you should not deny your practice at any time, for any reason.

An attorney experienced in business law can give you important information regarding the risks unique to your practice. Furthermore, the lawyer can advise you regarding your rights and obligations in your relationship with present and future employees, the rules that apply in your state regarding the hiring and firing of employees, permissible collection practices, and so forth. Ignorance of these issues and violation of the rules can result in financially devastating lawsuits and even criminal penalties. Each state has its own laws covering certain business practices; thus state laws must be consulted on many areas covered in this book. A competent local business attorney is your best source of information on many issues that will arise in the running of your practice.

What is really behind all the hoopla about preventive legal counseling? Are we lawyers simply seeking more work? Admittedly, as businesspeople, lawyers want business. But what you should consider is economic reality: *Just like medical problems, most legal problems cost more to solve or defend after they arise than it would have cost to prevent their occurrence in the first place.* Litigation is notoriously inefficient and expensive. You do not want to sue or be sued if you can help it. The expense is shocking; for instance, it can cost close to $100 per day simply to use a courtroom for trial. Pretrial procedures run into thousands of dollars in most cases. The cost of defending a case filed against you or your practice is something you have no choice but to incur unless you choose to default, which is almost never advisable.

The lawyer who will be most valuable to your young practice will likely not be a Raymond Burr or Robert Redford character, but rather a meticulous person who does most of his or her work in an office, going over your business forms, your employee contracts, or your corporate bylaws. This person should have a good reputation in the legal community as well as in the business community. You might pay over $150 per hour for the attorney, but if the firm has a good reputation it likely employs a well-trained professional staff that can reduce the amount of attorney time required.

One of the first items you should discuss with your lawyer is the fee structure. You are entitled to an estimate, though unless you enter into an agreement to the contrary with the attorney, the estimate is just that. Business lawyers generally charge by the hour, although you may be quoted a flat rate for a specific service such as incorporation or a real estate closing.

Finding a Lawyer

If you do not know any attorneys, ask other medical professionals whether they know any good ones. You want either a lawyer who specializes in business, or a general practitioner who has many happy business clients. Finding the lawyer who is right for you is like finding the right doctor; you may have to shop around a bit. Your city, county, and state bar associations may have helpful referral services. A good tip is to find out who is in the business law section of the state or county bar association or who has served on special committees dealing with business or health care law. It also may be useful to find out whether any articles covering the area of law you are concerned with have been published in either scholarly journals or continuing legal education publications, and if the author is available to assist you. It is a good idea to hire a specialist, or law firm with a number of specialists, rather than a general practitioner. While it is true that you may pay more per hour for the expert, you will not have to fund his learning time, and experience is valuable. In this regard, you may wish to keep in mind that it is uncommon for a lawyer to specialize in business practice and also handle criminal matters. Thus if you are faced with a criminal prosecution for drunk driving, you should be searching for an experienced criminal defense lawyer.

One method by which you can attempt to evaluate an attorney in regard to representing business clients is by consulting the *Martindale-Hubbell Law Directory* in your local county law library. While this may be useful, the mere fact that an attorney's name does not appear in the book should not be given too much weight, since there is a charge for being included, and some lawyers may have chosen not to pay for the listing.

After you have been given or have obtained several recommendations about attorneys, it is appropriate for you to talk with them for a short period of time to determine whether you would be comfortable working with them. Do not be afraid to ask about their experience, and whether they feel they can help you. Some lawyers will bill you for the initial consultation, so be sure to determine this when making your appointment.

Once you have completed the interview process, select the person who appears to best satisfy your needs. The rest is up to you. Contact your lawyer whenever you believe a legal question has arisen. Your attorney should aid you in identifying which questions require legal action or advice and which require business decisions. Generally, lawyers will deal only with legal issues, though they may help you to evaluate business problems.

I encourage my clients to feel comfortable about calling me at the office during the day or at home in the evening. However, some lawyers may resent having their personal time invaded. Some, in fact, do not list their home telephone number. You should learn your attorney's preference early on.

The attorney–client relationship is such that you should feel comfortable when confiding in your attorney. This person will not disclose your confidential communications; in fact, a violation of this rule, depending on the circumstances, can be considered an ethical breach that could subject the attorney to professional sanctions.

If you take the time to develop a good working relationship with your attorney, it may well prove to be one of your more valuable business assets.

Finding an Accountant

In addition to an attorney, most medical practitioners will need the services of a competent accountant to aid with tax planning and the filing of periodic and annual tax returns. Finding a CPA with whom your practice is compatible is similar to finding an attorney. You should ask around and learn which accountants are servicing practices similar to yours. State professional accounting associations may also provide a referral service or point you to a directory of accountants in your region. You should interview prospective accountants to determine whether you feel you can work with them and whether you feel their skill will be compatible with your practice needs.

As with your attorney, your accountant can provide valuable assistance in planning for the future of your practice. It is important to work with professionals you trust and with whom you are able to relate on a professional level.

Index

About the Author

Leonard D. DuBoff has been a legal educator for more than two decades, first as a Teaching Fellow at Stanford University Law School in Palo Alto, California, and then as a Professor of Law at Lewis and Clark Law School in Portland, Oregon. Beginning his legal practice in New York and continuing that practice throughout his career, he is now counsel to the Portland law firm of Cooney & Crew, P.C., which, among other specialties, focuses on representing doctors, dentists, hospitals, and others involved in the medical and dental professions. Indeed, the firm serves as outside counsel for the Oregon Medical Association, and one of the lawyers is the former Vice President/ General Counsel of the Oregon Association of Hospitals. Other books by Professor DuBoff include *The Law (in Plain English)® for Craftspeople*, third edition; *Business and Legal Forms (in Plain English)® for Craftspeople*; *The Law (in Plain English)® for Small Businesses*, second edition; *The Law (in Plain English)® for Writers*, second edition; *The Photographers' Business and Legal Handbook*; *The Book Publishers' Legal Guide*, second edition; *The Desk Book of Art Law*, second edition; *Art Law in a Nutshell*, second edition; *Law and the Visual Arts*; *Art Law: Domestic and International*; *High-Tech Law (in Plain English)®: An Entrepreneur's Guide*; and *The Crafts Business Encyclopedia*.